D0686177

# The Fact of a
# Doorframe

BY ADRIENNE RICH

Fox: Poems 1998–2000

Arts of the Possible: Essays and Conversations

Midnight Salvage: Poems 1995–1998

Dark Fields of the Republic: Poems 1991–1995

What Is Found There: Notebooks on Poetry and Politics

Collected Early Poems 1950–1970

An Atlas of the Difficult World: Poems 1988–1991

Time's Power: Poems 1985–1988

Blood, Bread, and Poetry: Selected Prose 1979–1985

Your Native Land, Your Life: Poems

Sources

A Wild Patience Has Taken Me This Far: Poems 1978–1981

On Lies, Secrets, and Silence: Selected Prose 1966–1978

The Dream of a Common Language: Poems 1974–1977

Twenty-one Love Poems

Of Woman Born: Motherhood as Experience and Institution

Poems: Selected and New, 1950–1974

Diving into the Wreck: Poems 1971–1972

The Will to Change

Leaflets

Necessities of Life

Snapshots of a Daughter-in-Law

The Diamond Cutters

A Change of World

# ADRIENNE RICH

# *The Fact of a Doorframe*

## Selected Poems 1950–2001

W. W. Norton & Company
New York   London

Copyright © 2002 by Adrienne Rich
Copyright © 2001, 1999, 1995, 1991, 1989, 1986, 1984, 1981, 1967, 1963, 1962,
1961, 1960, 1959, 1958, 1957, 1956, 1955, 1954, 1953, 1952, 1951 by Adrienne Rich
Copyright © 1978, 1975, 1973, 1971, 1969, 1966 by W. W. Norton & Company, Inc.

All rights reserved
Printed in the United States of America
For information about permission to reproduce selections from this book, write to
Permissions, W. W. Norton & Company, Inc., 500 Fifth Avenue, New York, NY 10110

The text of this book is composed in Times Roman, with display type set in Bodoni.
Composition by Julia Druskin
Manufacturing by The Haddon Craftsmen, Inc.
Production manager: Amanda Morrison

Library of Congress Cataloging-in-Publication Data

Rich, Adrienne Cecile.
    The fact of a doorframe : selected poems 1950–2001 / Adrienne Rich.
        p. cm.
    Includes index.
    **ISBN 0-393-32395-1 (pbk.)**
        I. Title.

PS3535.I233 A6 2002
811'.54—dc21

                                                                2002141447


W. W. Norton & Company, Inc., 500 Fifth Avenue, New York, N.Y. 10110
www.wwnorton.com


W. W. Norton & Company Ltd., Castle House, 75/76 Wells Street, London W1T 3QT

2 3 4 5 6 7 8 9 0

*for my teachers—present and gone*

# Contents

# From *Leaflets* (1969)

# From *The Will to Change* (1971)

## From *Diving into the Wreck* (1973)

## Uncollected Poems (1950–1974)

## From *The Dream of a Common Language* (1978)

# From *A Wild Patience Has Taken Me This Far* (1981)

# From *Your Native Land, Your Life* (1986)

# From *Time's Power* (1989)

## From *An Atlas of the Difficult World* (1991)

## From *Dark Fields of the Republic* (1995)

## From *Midnight Salvage* (1999)

## From *Fox* (2001)

# Foreword

A poem may be written in the moment but it does its work in time. May be written in acute emotion yet drives toward precision, compression, the existential intentionality of art which is its way of discovering meaning. Made in and from the material of language, poetry is continually wrestling with its own medium.

The language of any poem is the language of a society and the poet's relation to that society is implicit—or naked—in the poem: in image and metaphor, in traditions invoked or contended against, urgency or relaxation of the breath, musics listened to, echoes of conversations overheard, the entire complex of choices made, along with the subterranean dimension in all art.

These are some of the things you learn, as a poet, through practise and experience—working on your own poems, reading and pondering other poems and poetries, plunging your hands deep into the social language into which you were born, and other social languages you go on to experience.

In the title poem of this collection, written in 1974 (when earthquakes were still merely metaphorical to me) I spoke of poetry as "hewn from the commonest living substance" as a doorframe is hewn of wood. Later, I would define "the true nature of poetry" as "the drive to connect. / The dream of a common language." As time went on, I was to realize that "common" in the sense of collectively owned, is only relative where language is concerned. My given language was Anglo-American, threaded as it is with Africanisms, Creolisms, Spanish, Native American languages, each intimating a world and a history of its own.

Language as material force—this is something the student poet of *A Change of World* had not yet thought about, and twenty years later was impelled to reflect on in "The Burning of Paper Instead of Children." "I grasp for you," says the poet in "The Fact of a Doorframe," speaking to poetry itself, as language. "This is the oppressor's language," she wrote in "The Burning of Paper," "yet I need it to talk to you." A typewriter in flames is the metaphor here. To work in a medium which can be, has been, used as an instrument of trivialization and deceit, not to mention colonization and humiliation, is somewhat different from working in a medium like stone, clay, paint, charcoal, even iron or steel. A poet cannot refuse language, choose another medium. But the poet can re-fuse the language given to him or her, bend and torque it into an instrument for connection instead of dominance and apartheid: toward what Edouard Glissant has wonderfully called "the poetics of relation." The anarchist poet Paul Goodman wrote of "the gaunt and fumbling style of acting out of desperation." Poetry has need for this style, as well as for the luminosity of the lyrical phrase, the Whitmanic or Biblical measure of the ocean, impetuosity and wit, the dialogic phrasing of jazz, moments of delicacy on the edges of silence—and much else. What poetry does not need is conformity and complacency.

My life has been enmeshed so long with poetry that I cannot, looking back at this collection of five decades, imagine how I would have survived without this doorframe, this work. But it was first the poetry of others, in English—Blake, Keats, Longfellow, Robert Louis Stevenson, Swinburne, Oscar Wilde, the King James version of the Bible—listened to and read in childhood, that let me know the doorframe was there for me, that such a possibility existed. And there were the rhythms of everyday sayings and rhymes and narration, songs sung at the living-room piano, my parents' Southern tonalities, African American talk, speeches on the radio during World War II. You can absorb all this and still not know what, literally, to make of it. Whatever I have come to make of it I owe to these early, certainly privileged beginnings and to my later awakening to the power and responsibilities of the art—through the poems of my contemporaries, through friends, teachers, lovers, and students, through political movements, and of course through mistakes and accidental turnings.

I want to thank my editor, Jill Bialosky, my literary agent, Frances Goldin, my lecture agent, Steven Barclay, all of whom, with their colleagues, have given my work extraordinary and skillful support.

Adrienne Rich
March 2002

From

*A Change of World*

1951

# Storm Warnings

The glass has been falling all the afternoon,
And knowing better than the instrument
What winds are walking overhead, what zone
Of gray unrest is moving across the land,
I leave the book upon a pillowed chair
And walk from window to closed window, watching
Boughs strain against the sky

And think again, as often when the air
Moves inward toward a silent core of waiting,
How with a single purpose time has traveled
By secret currents of the undiscerned
Into this polar realm. Weather abroad
And weather in the heart alike come on
Regardless of prediction.

Between foreseeing and averting change
Lies all the mastery of elements
Which clocks and weatherglasses cannot alter.
Time in the hand is not control of time,
Nor shattered fragments of an instrument
A proof against the wind; the wind will rise,
We can only close the shutters.

I draw the curtains as the sky goes black
And set a match to candles sheathed in glass
Against the keyhole draught, the insistent whine
Of weather through the unsealed aperture.
This is our sole defense against the season;
These are the things that we have learned to do
Who live in troubled regions.

# Aunt Jennifer's Tigers

Aunt Jennifer's tigers prance across a screen,
Bright topaz denizens of a world of green.
They do not fear the men beneath the tree;
They pace in sleek chivalric certainty.

Aunt Jennifer's fingers fluttering through her wool
Find even the ivory needle hard to pull.
The massive weight of Uncle's wedding band
Sits heavily upon Aunt Jennifer's hand.

When Aunt is dead, her terrified hands will lie
Still ringed with ordeals she was mastered by.
The tigers in the panel that she made
Will go on prancing, proud and unafraid.

# Boundary

What has happened here will do
To bite the living world in two,
Half for me and half for you.
Here at last I fix a line
Severing the world's design
Too small to hold both yours and mine.
There's enormity in a hair
Enough to lead men not to share
Narrow confines of a sphere
But put an ocean or a fence
Between two opposite intents.
A hair would span the difference.

# At a Bach Concert

Coming by evening through the wintry city
We said that art is out of love with life.
Here we approach a love that is not pity.

This antique discipline, tenderly severe,
Renews belief in love yet masters feeling,
Asking of us a grace in what we bear.

Form is the ultimate gift that love can offer—
The vital union of necessity
With all that we desire, all that we suffer.

A too-compassionate art is half an art.
Only such proud restraining purity
Restores the else-betrayed, too-human heart.

From

# *The Diamond Cutters*

1955

# Ideal Landscape

We had to take the world as it was given:
The nursemaid sitting passive in the park
Was rarely by a changeling prince accosted.
The mornings happened similar and stark
In rooms of selfhood where we woke and lay
Watching today unfold like yesterday.

Our friends were not unearthly beautiful,
Nor spoke with tongues of gold; our lovers blundered
Now and again when most we sought perfection,
Or hid in cupboards when the heavens thundered.
The human rose to haunt us everywhere,
Raw, flawed, and asking more than we could bear.

And always time was rushing like a tram
Through streets of a foreign city, streets we saw
Opening into great and sunny squares
We could not find again, no map could show—
Never those fountains tossed in that same light,
Those gilded trees, those statues green and white.


# Living in Sin

She had thought the studio would keep itself;
no dust upon the furniture of love.
Half heresy, to wish the taps less vocal,
the panes relieved of grime. A plate of pears,
a piano with a Persian shawl, a cat
stalking the picturesque amusing mouse

        •

had risen at his urging.
Not that at five each separate stair would writhe
under the milkman's tramp; that morning light
so coldly would delineate the scraps
of last night's cheese and three sepulchral bottles;
that on the kitchen shelf among the saucers
a pair of beetle-eyes would fix her own—
envoy from some village in the moldings . . .
Meanwhile, he, with a yawn,
sounded a dozen notes upon the keyboard,
declared it out of tune, shrugged at the mirror,
rubbed at his beard, went out for cigarettes;
while she, jeered by the minor demons,
pulled back the sheets and made the bed and found
a towel to dust the table-top,
and let the coffee-pot boil over on the stove.
By evening she was back in love again,
though not so wholly but throughout the night
she woke sometimes to feel the daylight coming
like a relentless milkman up the stairs.

# The Snow Queen

Child with a chip of mirror in his eye
Saw the world ugly, fled to plains of ice
Where beauty was the Snow Queen's promises.
Under my lids a splinter sharp as his
Has made me wish you lying dead
Whose image digs the needle deeper still.

In the deceptive province of my birth
I had seen yes turn no, the saints descend,
Their sacred faces twisted into smiles,
The stars gone lechering, the village spring

Gush mud and toads—all miracles
Befitting an incalculable age.

To love a human face was to discover
The cracks of paint and varnish on the brow;
Soon to distrust all impulses of flesh
That strews its sawdust on the chamber floor,
While at the window peer two crones
Who once were Juliet and Jessica.

No matter, since I kept a little while
One thing intact from that perversity—
Though landscapes bloomed in monstrous cubes and coils.
In you belonged simplicities of light
To mend distraction, teach the air
To shine, the stars to find their way again.

Yet here the Snow Queen's cold prodigious will
Commands me, and your face has lost its power,
Dissolving to its opposite like the rest.
Under my ribs a diamond splinter now
Sticks, and has taken root; I know
Only this frozen spear that drives me through.


# Letter from the Land of Sinners

I write you this out of another province
That you may never see:
Country of rivers, its topography
Mutable in detail, yet always one,
Blasted in certain places, here by glaciers,
There by the work of man.
        •

The fishers by the water have no boast
Save of their freedom; here
A man may cast a dozen kinds of lure
And think his days rewarded if he sight
Now and again the prize, unnetted, flicking
Its prism-gleams of light.

The old lord lived secluded in his park
Until the hall was burned
Years ago, by his tenants; both have learned
Better since then, and now our children run
To greet him. Quail and hunter have forgotten
The echo of the gun.

I said there are blasted places: we have kept
Their nakedness intact—
No marble to commemorate an act
Superhuman or merely rash; we know
Why they are there and why the seed that falls there
Is certain not to grow.

We keep these places as we keep the time
Scarred on our recollection
When some we loved broke from us in defection,
Or we ourselves harried to death too soon
What we could least forgo. Our memories
Recur like the old moon.

But we have made another kind of peace,
And walk where boughs are green,
Forgiven by the selves that we have been,
And learning to forgive. Our apples taste
Sweeter this year; our gates are falling down,
And need not be replaced.

From

*Snapshots of a Daughter-in-Law*

1963

# From Morning-Glory to Petersburg

(*The World Book,* 1928)

"Organized knowledge in story and picture"
    confronts through dusty glass
    an eye grown dubious.
I can recall when knowledge still was pure,
    not contradictory, pleasurable
    as cutting out a paper doll.
You opened up a book and there it was:
    everything just as promised, from
    Kurdistan to Mormons, Gum
Arabic to Kumquat, neither more nor less.
    Facts could be kept separate
    by a convention; that was what
made childhood possible. Now knowledge finds me out;
    in all its risible untidiness
    it traces me to each address,
dragging in things I never thought about.
    I don't invite what facts can be
    held at arm's length; a family
of jeering irresponsibles always
    comes along gypsy-style
    and there you have them all
forever on your hands. It never pays.
    If I could still extrapolate
    the morning-glory on the gate
from Petersburg in history—but it's too late.

1954

# The Knight

A knight rides into the noon,
and his helmet points to the sun,
and a thousand splintered suns
are the gaiety of his mail.
The soles of his feet glitter
and his palms flash in reply,
and under his crackling banner
he rides like a ship in sail.

A knight rides into the noon,
and only his eye is living,
a lump of bitter jelly
set in a metal mask,
betraying rags and tatters
that cling to the flesh beneath
and wear his nerves to ribbons
under the radiant casque.

Who will unhorse this rider
and free him from between
the walls of iron, the emblems
crushing his chest with their weight?
Will they defeat him gently,
or leave him hurled on the green,
his rags and wounds still hidden
under the great breastplate?

1957

# Snapshots of a Daughter-in-Law

1.

You, once a belle in Shreveport,
with henna-colored hair, skin like a peachbud,
still have your dresses copied from that time,
and play a Chopin prelude
called by Cortot: *"Delicious recollections
float like perfume through the memory."*

Your mind now, moldering like wedding-cake,
heavy with useless experience, rich
with suspicion, rumor, fantasy,
crumbling to pieces under the knife-edge
of mere fact. In the prime of your life.

Nervy, glowering, your daughter
wipes the teaspoons, grows another way.

2.

Banging the coffee-pot into the sink
she hears the angels chiding, and looks out
past the raked gardens to the sloppy sky.
Only a week since They said: *Have no patience.*

The next time it was: *Be insatiable.*
Then: *Save yourself; others you cannot save.*
Sometimes she's let the tapstream scald her arm,
a match burn to her thumbnail,

•

or held her hand above the kettle's snout
right in the woolly steam. They are probably angels,
since nothing hurts her anymore, except
each morning's grit blowing into her eyes.


3.


A thinking woman sleeps with monsters.
The beak that grips her, she becomes. And Nature,
that sprung-lidded, still commodious
steamer-trunk of *tempora* and *mores*
gets stuffed with it all:      the mildewed orange-flowers,
the female pills, the terrible breasts
of Boadicea beneath flat foxes' heads and orchids.

Two handsome women, gripped in argument,
each proud, acute, subtle, I hear scream
across the cut glass and majolica
like Furies cornered from their prey:
The argument *ad feminam,* all the old knives
that have rusted in my back, I drive in yours,
*ma semblable, ma soeur!*


4.


Knowing themselves too well in one another:
their gifts no pure fruition, but a thorn,
the prick filed sharp against a hint of scorn . . .
Reading while waiting
for the iron to heat,
writing, *My Life had stood—a Loaded Gun—*
in that Amherst pantry while the jellies boil and scum,
or, more often,
iron-eyed and beaked and purposed as a bird,
dusting everything on the whatnot every day of life.
                    •

5.

*Dulce ridens, dulce loquens,*
she shaves her legs until they gleam
like petrified mammoth-tusk.

6.

When to her lute Corinna sings
neither words nor music are her own;
only the long hair dipping
over her cheek, only the song
of silk against her knees
and these
adjusted in reflections of an eye.

Poised, trembling and unsatisfied, before
an unlocked door, that cage of cages,
tell us, you bird, you tragical machine—
is this *fertilisante douleur?* Pinned down
by love, for you the only natural action,
are you edged more keen
to prise the secrets of the vault? has Nature shown
her household books to you, daughter-in-law,
that her sons never saw?

7.

*"To have in this uncertain world some stay*
*which cannot be undermined, is*
*of the utmost consequence."*
                                    Thus wrote
a woman, partly brave and partly good,
who fought with what she partly understood.
Few men about her would or could do more,
hence she was labeled harpy, shrew and whore.
        •

8.

"You all die at fifteen," said Diderot,
and turn part legend, part convention.
Still, eyes inaccurately dream
behind closed windows blankening with steam.
Deliciously, all that we might have been,
all that we were—fire, tears,
wit, taste, martyred ambition—
stirs like the memory of refused adultery
the drained and flagging bosom of our middle years.

9.

*Not that it is done well, but
that it is done at all?* Yes, think
of the odds! or shrug them off forever.
This luxury of the precocious child,
Time's precious chronic invalid,—
would we, darlings, resign it if we could?
Our blight has been our sinecure:
mere talent was enough for us—
glitter in fragments and rough drafts.

Sigh no more, ladies.
                    Time is male
and in his cups drinks to the fair.
Bemused by gallantry, we hear
our mediocrities over-praised,
indolence read as abnegation,
slattern thought styled intuition,
every lapse forgiven, our crime
only to cast too bold a shadow
or smash the mold straight off.

For that, solitary confinement,
tear gas, attrition shelling.
Few applicants for that honor.
            •

10.

                    Well,
she's long about her coming, who must be
more merciless to herself than history.
Her mind full to the wind, I see her plunge
breasted and glancing through the currents,
taking the light upon her
at least as beautiful as any boy
or helicopter,
                    poised, still coming,
her fine blades making the air wince

but her cargo
no promise then:
delivered
palpable
ours.

1958–1960


# Antinoüs: The Diaries

Autumn torture. The old signs
smeared on the pavement, sopping leaves
rubbed into the landscape as unguent on a bruise,
brought indoors, even, as they bring flowers, enormous,
with the colors of the body's secret parts.
All this. And then, evenings, needing to be out,
walking fast, fighting the fire
that must die, light that sets my teeth on edge with joy,
till on the black embankment
I'm a cart stopped in the ruts of time.
        •

Then at some house the rumor of truth and beauty
saturates a room like lilac-water
in the steam of a bath, fires snap, heads are high,
gold hair at napes of necks, gold in glasses,
gold in the throat, poetry of furs and manners.
Why do I shiver then? Haven't I seen,
over and over, before the end of an evening,
the three opened coffins carried in and left in a corner?
Haven't I watched as somebody cracked his shin
on one of them, winced and hopped and limped
laughing to lay his hand on a beautiful arm
striated with hairs of gold, like an almond-shell?

The old, needless story. For if I'm here
it is by choice and when at last
I smell my own rising nausea, feel the air
tighten around my stomach like a surgical bandage,
I can't pretend surprise. What is it I so miscarry?
If what I spew on the tiles at last,
helpless, disgraced, alone,
is in part what I've swallowed from glasses, eyes,
motions of hands, opening and closing mouths,
isn't it also dead gobbets of myself,
abortive, murdered, or never willed?

1959



# Peeling Onions

Only to have a grief
equal to all these tears!

There's not a sob in my chest.
Dry-hearted as Peer Gynt
                •

I pare away, no hero,
merely a cook.

Crying was labor, once
when I'd good cause.
Walking, I felt my eyes like wounds
raw in my head,
so postal-clerks, I thought, must stare.
A dog's look, a cat's, burnt to my brain—
yet all that stayed
stuffed in my lungs like smog.

These old tears in the chopping-bowl.

1961

# The Roofwalker

*—for Denise Levertov*

Over the half-finished houses
night comes. The builders
stand on the roof. It is
quiet after the hammers,
the pulleys hang slack.
Giants, the roofwalkers,
on a listing deck, the wave
of darkness about to break
on their heads. The sky
is a torn sail where figures
pass magnified, shadows
on a burning deck.

I feel like them up there:
exposed, larger than life,
and due to break my neck.

Was it worth while to lay—
with infinite exertion—
a roof I can't live under?
—All those blueprints,
closings of gaps,
measurings, calculations?
A life I didn't choose
chose me: even
my tools are the wrong ones
for what I have to do.
I'm naked, ignorant,
a naked man fleeing
across the roofs
who could with a shade of difference
be sitting in the lamplight
against the cream wallpaper
reading—not with indifference—
about a naked man
fleeing across the roofs.

1961


# Prospective Immigrants Please Note

Either you will
go through this door
or you will not go through.

If you go through
there is always the risk
of remembering your name.
                •

Things look at you doubly
and you must look back
and let them happen.

If you do not go through
it is possible
to live worthily

to maintain your attitudes
to hold your position
to die bravely

but much will blind you,
much will evade you,
at what cost who knows?

The door itself
makes no promises.
It is only a door.

1962

From

*Necessities of Life*

1966

# Necessities of Life

Piece by piece I seem
to re-enter the world: I first began

a small, fixed dot, still see
that old myself, a dark-blue thumbtack

pushed into the scene,
a hard little head protruding

from the pointillist's buzz and bloom.
After a time the dot

begins to ooze. Certain heats
melt it.
   Now I was hurriedly

blurring into ranges
of burnt red, burning green,

whole biographies swam up and
swallowed me like Jonah.

Jonah! I was Wittgenstein,
Mary Wollstonecraft, the soul

of Louis Jouvet, dead
in a blown-up photograph.

Till, wolfed almost to shreds,
I learned to make myself

  •

unappetizing. Scaly as a dry bulb
thrown into a cellar

I used myself, let nothing use me.
Like being on a private dole,

sometimes more like kneading bricks in Egypt.
What life was there, was mine,

now and again to lay
one hand on a warm brick

and touch the sun's ghost
with economical joy,

now and again to name
over the bare necessities.

So much for those days. Soon
practice may make me middling-perfect, I'll

dare inhabit the world
trenchant in motion as an eel, solid

as a cabbage-head. I have invitations:
a curl of mist steams upward

from a field, visible as my breath,
houses along a road stand waiting

like old women knitting, breathless
to tell their tales.

1962

# In the Woods

"Difficult ordinary happiness,"
no one nowadays believes in you.
I shift, full-length on the blanket,
to fix the sun precisely

behind the pine-tree's crest
so light spreads through the needles
alive as water just
where a snake has surfaced,

unreal as water in green crystal.
Bad news is always arriving.
"We're hiders, hiding from something bad,"
sings the little boy.

Writing these words in the woods,
I feel like a traitor to my friends,
even to my enemies.
The common lot's to die

a stranger's death and lie
rouged in the coffin, in a dress
chosen by the funeral director.
Perhaps that's why we never

see clocks on public buildings any more.
A fact no architect will mention.
We're hiders, hiding from something bad
most of the time.

Yet, and outrageously, something good
finds us, found me this morning
        •

lying on a dusty blanket
among the burnt-out Indian pipes

and bursting-open lady's-slippers.
My soul, my helicopter, whirred
distantly, by habit, over
the old pond with the half-drowned boat

toward which it always veers
for consolation: ego's Arcady:
leaving the body stuck
like a leaf against a screen.—

Happiness! how many times
I've stranded on that word,
at the edge of that pond; seen
as if through tears, the dragon-fly—

only to find it all
going differently for once
this time: my soul wheeled back
and burst into my body.

Found! Ready or not.
If I move now, the sun
naked between the trees
will melt me as I lie.

1963

# The Trees

The trees inside are moving out into the forest,
the forest that was empty all these days
where no bird could sit
no insect hide
no sun bury its feet in shadow
the forest that was empty all these nights
will be full of trees by morning.

All night the roots work
to disengage themselves from the cracks
in the veranda floor.
The leaves strain toward the glass
small twigs stiff with exertion
long-cramped boughs shuffling under the roof
like newly discharged patients
half-dazed, moving
to the clinic doors.

I sit inside, doors open to the veranda
writing long letters
in which I scarcely mention the departure
of the forest from the house.
The night is fresh, the whole moon shines
in a sky still open
the smell of leaves and lichen
still reaches like a voice into the rooms.
My head is full of whispers
which tomorrow will be silent.

Listen. The glass is breaking.
The trees are stumbling forward
into the night. Winds rush to meet them.
                •

The moon is broken like a mirror,
its pieces flash now in the crown
of the tallest oak.

1963

# Like This Together

*—for A.H.C.*

1.

Wind rocks the car.
We sit parked by the river,
silence between our teeth.
Birds scatter across islands
of broken ice. Another time
I'd have said: "Canada geese,"
knowing you love them.
A year, ten years from now
I'll remember this—
this sitting like drugged birds
in a glass case—
not why, only that we
were here like this together.

2.

They're tearing down, tearing up
this city, block by block.
Rooms cut in half
hang like flayed carcasses,
their old roses in rags,
famous streets have forgotten
where they were going. Only

•

a fact could be so dreamlike.
They're tearing down the houses
we met and lived in,
soon our two bodies will be all
left standing from that era.

3.

We have, as they say,
certain things in common.
I mean: a view
from a bathroom window
over slate to stiff pigeons
huddled every morning; the way
water tastes from our tap,
which you marvel at, letting
it splash into the glass.
Because of you I notice
the taste of water,
a luxury I might
otherwise have missed.

4.

Our words misunderstand us.
Sometimes at night
you are my mother:
old detailed griefs
twitch at my dreams, and I
crawl against you, fighting
for shelter, making you
my cave. Sometimes
you're the wave of birth
that drowns me in my first
nightmare. I suck the air.
Miscarried knowledge twists us
like hot sheets thrown askew.
                    •

5.

Dead winter doesn't die,
it wears away, a piece of carrion
picked clean at last,
rained away or burnt dry.
Our desiring does this,
make no mistake, I'm speaking
of fact: through mere indifference
we could prevent it.
Only our fierce attention
gets hyacinths out of those
hard cerebral lumps,
unwraps the wet buds down
the whole length of a stem.

1963

# Night-Pieces: For a Child

1. *The Crib*

You sleeping I bend to cover.
Your eyelids work. I see
your dream, cloudy as a negative,
swimming underneath.
You blurt a cry. Your eyes
spring open, still filmed in dream.
Wider, they fix me—
—death's head, sphinx, medusa?
You scream.
Tears lick my cheeks, my knees
droop at your fear.
Mother I no more am,
but woman, and nightmare.

2. *Her Waking*

Tonight I jerk astart in a dark
hourless as Hiroshima,
almost hearing you breathe
in a cot three doors away.

You still breathe, yes—
and my dream with its gift of knives,
its murderous hider and seeker,
ebbs away, recoils

back into the egg of dreams,
the vanishing point of mind.
All gone.

But you and I—
swaddled in a dumb dark
old as sickheartedness,
modern as pure annihilation—

we drift in ignorance.
If I could hear you now
mutter some gentle animal sound!
If milk flowed from my breast again. . . .

1964

# "I Am in Danger—Sir—"

"Half-cracked" to Higginson, living,
afterward famous in garbled versions,
your hoard of dazzling scraps a battlefield,
now your old snood

mothballed at Harvard
and you in your variorum monument
equivocal to the end—
who are you?

Gardening the day-lily,
wiping the wine-glass stems,
your thought pulsed on behind
a forehead battered paper-thin,

you, woman, masculine
in single-mindedness,
for whom the word was more
than a symptom—

a condition of being.
Till the air buzzing with spoiled language
sang in your ears
of Perjury

and in your half-cracked way you chose
silence for entertainment,
chose to have it out at last
on your own premises.

1964

# Mourning Picture

*The picture was painted by Edwin Romanzo Elmer*
*(1850–1923) as a memorial to his daughter Effie.*
*In the poem, it is the dead girl who speaks.*

They have carried the mahogany chair and the cane rocker
out under the lilac bush,
and my father and mother darkly sit there, in black clothes.
Our clapboard house stands fast on its hill,
my doll lies in her wicker pram
gazing at western Massachusetts.
This was our world.
I could remake each shaft of grass
feeling its rasp on my fingers,
draw out the map of every lilac leaf
or the net of veins on my father's
grief-tranced hand.

Out of my head, half-bursting,
still filling, the dream condenses—
shadows, crystals, ceilings, meadows, globes of dew.
Under the dull green of the lilacs, out in the light
carving each spoke of the pram, the turned porch-pillars
under high early-summer clouds,
I am Effie, visible and invisible,
remembering and remembered.

They will move from the house,
give the toys and pets away.
Mute and rigid with loss my mother
will ride the train to Baptist Corner,
the silk-spool will run bare.
I tell you, the thread that bound us lies
•

faint as a web in the dew.
Should I make you, world, again,
could I give back the leaf its skeleton, the air
its early-summer cloud, the house
its noonday presence, shadowless,
and leave *this* out? I am Effie, you were my dream.

1965


# The Knot


In the heart of the queen anne's lace, a knot of blood.
For years I never saw it,

years of metallic vision,
spears glancing off a bright eyeball,

suns off a Swiss lake.
A foaming meadow; the Milky Way;

and there, all along, the tiny dark-red spider
sitting in the whiteness of the bridal web,

waiting to plunge his crimson knifepoint
into the white apparencies.

Little wonder the eye, healing, sees
for a long time through a mist of blood.

1965

# Focus

—*for Bert Dreyfus*

Obscurity has its tale to tell.
Like the figure on the studio-bed in the corner,

out of range, smoking, watching and waiting.
Sun pours through the skylight onto the worktable

making of a jar of pencils, a typewriter keyboard
more than they were. Veridical light . . .

Earth budges. Now an empty coffee-cup,
a whetstone, a handkerchief, take on

their sacramental clarity, fixed by the wand
of light as the thinker thinks to fix them in the mind.

O secret in the core of the whetstone, in the five
pencils splayed out like fingers of a hand!

The mind's passion is all for singling out.
Obscurity has another tale to tell.

1965

# From

## *Leaflets*

1969

# Orion

Far back when I went zig-zagging
through tamarack pastures
you were my genius, you
my cast-iron Viking, my helmed
lion-heart king in prison.
Years later now you're young

my fierce half-brother, staring
down from that simplified west
your breast open, your belt dragged down
by an oldfashioned thing, a sword
the last bravado you won't give over
though it weighs you down as you stride

and the stars in it are dim
and maybe have stopped burning.
But you burn, and I know it;
as I throw back my head to take you in
an old transfusion happens again:
divine astronomy is nothing to it.

Indoors I bruise and blunder,
break faith, leave ill enough
alone, a dead child born in the dark.
Night cracks up over the chimney,
pieces of time, frozen geodes
come showering down in the grate.

A man reaches behind my eyes
and finds them empty
a woman's head turns away
from my head in the mirror
                    •

children are dying my death
and eating crumbs of my life.

Pity is not your forte.
Calmly you ache up there
pinned aloft in your crow's nest,
my speechless pirate!
You take it all for granted
and when I look you back

it's with a starlike eye
shooting its cold and egotistical spear
where it can do least damage.
Breathe deep! No hurt, no pardon
out here in the cold with you
you with your back to the wall.

1965


# In the Evening

Three hours chain-smoking words
and you move on. We stand in the porch,
two archaic figures: a woman and a man.

The old masters, the old sources,
haven't a clue what we're about,
shivering here in the half-dark 'sixties.

Our minds hover in a famous impasse
and cling together. Your hand
grips mine like a railing on an icy night.
                •

The wall of the house is bleeding. Firethorn!
The moon, cracked every-which-way,
pushes steadily on.

1966


# The Demon Lover

Fatigue, regrets. The lights
go out in the parking lot
two by two. Snow blindness
settles over the suburb.
Desire. Desire. The nebula
opens in space, unseen,
your heart utters its great beats
in solitude. A new
era is coming in.
Gauche as we are, it seems
we have to play our part.

A plaid dress, silk scarf,
and eyes that go on stinging.
Woman, stand off. The air
glistens like silk.
She's gone. In her place stands
a schoolgirl, morning light,
the half-grown bones
of innocence. Is she
your daughter or your muse,
this tree of blondness
grown up in a field of thorns?

Something piercing and marred.
Take note. Look back. When quick
    •

the whole northeast went black
and prisoners howled and children
ran through the night with candles,
who stood off motionless
side by side while the moon swam up
over the drowned houses?
Who neither touched nor spoke?
whose nape, whose finger-ends
nervelessly lied the hours away?

A voice presses at me.
If I give in it won't
be like the girl the bull rode,
all Rubens flesh and happy moans.
But to be wrestled like a boy
with tongue, hips, knees, nerves, brain . . .
with language?
He doesn't know. He's watching
breasts under a striped blouse,
his bull's head down. The old
wine pours again through my veins.

Goodnight. then. 'Night. Again
we turn our backs and weary
weary we let down.
Things take us hard, no question.
*How do you make it, all the way*
*from here to morning?* I touch
you, made of such nerve
and flare and pride and swallowed tears.
Go home. Come to bed. The skies
look in at us, stern.
And this is an old story.

I dreamed about the war.
We were all sitting at table
in a kitchen in Chicago.
The radio had just screamed

•

that Illinois was the target.
No one felt like leaving,
we sat by the open window
and talked in the sunset.
*I'll tell you that joke tomorrow,*
you said with your saddest smile,
*if I can remember.*

The end is just a straw,
a feather furling slowly down,
floating to light by chance, a breath
on the long-loaded scales.
Posterity trembles like a leaf
and we go on making heirs and heirlooms.
*The world, we have to make it,*
my coexistent friend said, leaning
back in his cell.
Siberia vastly hulks
behind him, which he did not make.

Oh futile tenderness
of touch in a world like this!
how much longer, dear child,
do you think sex will matter?
There might have been a wedding
that never was:
two creatures sprung free
from castiron covenants.
Instead our hands and minds
erotically waver . . .
Lightness is unavailing.

Catalpas wave and spill
their dull strings across this murk of spring.
I ache, brilliantly.
Only where there is language is there world.
In the harp of my hair, compose me
a song. Death's in the air,
        •

we all know that. Still, for an hour,
I'd like to be gay. How could a gay song go?
Why that's your secret, and it shall be mine.
We are our words, and black and bruised and blue.
Under our skins, we're laughing.

*In triste veritas?*
Take hold, sweet hands, come on . . .
Broken!
When you falter, all eludes.
This is a seasick way,
this almost/never touching, this
drawing-off, this to-and-fro.
Subtlety stalks in your eyes,
your tongue knows what it knows.
I want your secrets—I *will* have them out.
Seasick, I drop into the sea.

1966


# Jerusalem

In my dream, children
are stoning other children
with blackened carob-pods
I dream my son is riding
on an old grey mare
to a half-dead war
on a dead-grey road
through the cactus and thistles
and dried brook-beds.

In my dream, children
are swaddled in smoke

and their uncut hair smolders
even here, here
where trees have no shade
and rocks have no shadow
trees have no memories
only the stones and
the hairs of the head.

I dream his hair is growing
and has never been shorn
from slender temples hanging
like curls of barbed wire
and his first beard is growing
smoldering like fire
his beard is smoke and fire
and I dream him riding
patiently to the war.

What I dream of the city
is how hard it is to leave
and how useless to walk
outside the blasted walls
picking up the shells
from a half-dead war
and I wake up in tears
and hear the sirens screaming
and the carob-tree is bare.

*Balfour Street*
*July 1966*

# Night Watch

And now, outside, the walls
of black flint, eyeless.
How pale in sleep you lie.
Love: my love is just a breath
blown on the pane and dissolved.
Everything, even you,
cries silently for help, the web
of the spider is ripped with rain,
the geese fly on into the black cloud.
What can I do for you?
what can I do for you?
Can the touch of a finger mend
what a finger's touch has broken?
Blue-eyed now, yellow-haired,
I stand in my old nightmare
beside the track, while you,
and over and over and always you
plod into the deathcars.
Sometimes you smile at me
and I—I smile back at you.
How sweet the odor of the station-master's roses!
How pure, how poster-like the colors of this dream.

1967

# For a Russian Poet

1. *The winter dream*

Everywhere, snow is falling. Your bandaged foot
drags across huge cobblestones, bells
hammer in distant squares.
Everything we stood against has conquered
and now we're part
of it all. *Life's the main thing,* I hear you say,
but a fog is spreading between this landmass
and the one your voice
mapped so long for me. All that's visible
is walls, endlessly yellow-grey, where
so many risks were taken, the shredded skies
slowly littering both our continents with
the only justice left, burying
footprints, bells and voices with all deliberate speed.

1967

2. *Summer in the country*

Now, again, every year for years: the life-and-death talk,
late August, forebodings
under the birches, along the water's edge
and between the typed lines

and evenings, tracing a pattern of absurd hopes
in broken nutshells
                    but this year we both
sit after dark with the radio
unable to read, unable to write

    •

trying the blurred edges of broadcasts
for a little truth, taking a walk before bed
wondering what a man can do, asking that
at the verge of tears in a lightning-flash of loneliness


3. *The demonstration*

"Natalya Gorbanevskaya
13/3 Novopeschanaya Street
Apartment 34

At noon we sit down quietly on the parapet
and unfurl our banners
                              almost immediately
the sound of police whistles
from all corners of Red Square
                                        we sit
quietly and offer no resistance—"

Is this your little boy—?

we will relive this over and over

the banners torn
from our hands
                    blood flowing
a great jagged torn place
in the silence of complicity

that much at least
we did here

In your flat, drinking tea
waiting for the police
your children asleep while you write
quickly, the letters you want to get off
         •

before tomorrow

I'm a ghost at your table
touching poems in a script I can't read

we'll meet each other later

*August* 1968


# Abnegation

The red fox, the vixen
dancing in the half-light among the junipers,
wise-looking in a sexy way,
Egyptian-supple in her sharpness—
what does she want
with the dreams of dead vixens,
the apotheosis of Reynard,
the literature of fox-hunting?
Only in her nerves the past
sings, a thrill of self-preservation.
I go along down the road
to a house nailed together by Scottish
Covenanters, instinct mortified
in a virgin forest,
and she springs toward her den
every hair on her pelt alive
with tidings of the immaculate present.
They left me a westernness,
a birthright, a redstained, ravelled
afghan of sky.
She has no archives,
no heirlooms, no future
        •

except death
and I could be more
her sister than theirs
who chopped their way across these hills
—a chosen people.

1968


# Implosions

*The world's*
*not wanton*
*only wild and wavering*

I wanted to choose words that even you
would have to be changed by

Take the word
of my pulse, loving and ordinary
Send out your signals, hoist
your dark scribbled flags
but take
my hand

All wars are useless to the dead

My hands are knotted in the rope
and I cannot sound the bell

My hands are frozen to the switch
and I cannot throw it

The foot is in the wheel
            •

When it's finished and we're lying
in a stubble of blistered flowers
eyes gaping, mouths staring
dusted with crushed arterial blues

I'll have done nothing
even for you?


1968


# On Edges


When the ice starts to shiver
all across the reflecting basin
or water-lily leaves
dissect a simple surface
the word *drowning* flows through me.
You built a glassy floor
that held me
as I leaned to fish for old
hooks and toothed tin cans,
stems lashing out like ties of
silk dressing-gowns
archangels of lake-light
gripped in mud.

Now you hand me a torn letter.
On my knees, in the ashes, I could never
fit these ripped-up flakes together.
In the taxi I am still piecing
what syllables I can
translating at top speed like a thinking machine
that types out *useless* as *monster*
and *history* as *lampshade.*
    •

Crossing the bridge I need all my nerve
to trust to the man-made cables.

The blades on that machine
could cut you to ribbons
but its function is humane.
Is this all I can say of these
delicate hooks, scythe-curved intentions
you and I handle? I'd rather
taste blood, yours or mine, flowing
from a sudden slash, than cut all day
with blunt scissors on dotted lines
like the teacher told.

1968

# Leaflets

1.

The big star, and that other
lonely on black glass
overgrown with frozen
lesions, endless night
the Coal Sack gaping
black veins of ice on the pane
spelling a word:
            *Insomnia*
not manic but ordinary
to start out of sleep
turning off and on
this seasick neon
vision, this
division
            •

the head clears of sweet smoke
and poison gas

life without caution
the only worth living
love for a man
love for a woman
love for the facts
protectless

that self-defense be not
the arm's first motion

memory not only
cards of identity

*that I can live half a year*
*as I have never lived up to this time—*
Chekhov coughing up blood almost daily
the steamer edging in toward the penal colony
chained men dozing on deck
five forest fires lighting the island

lifelong that glare, waiting.


2.

Your face
            stretched like a mask
                          begins to tear
as you speak of Che Guevara
Bolivia, Nanterre
I'm too young to be your mother
you're too young to be my brother

your tears are not political
they are real water, burning
            •

as the tears of Telemachus
burned

Over Spanish Harlem the moon
swells up, a fire balloon
fire gnawing the edge
of this crushed-up newspaper

                              now

the bodies come whirling
coal-black, ash-white
out of torn windows
and the death columns blacken
                         whispering
*Who'd choose this life?*

We're fighting for a slash of recognition,
a piercing to the pierced heart.
*Tell me what you are going through—*

but the attention flickers and will flicker
a matchflame in poison air
a thread, a hair of light: sum of all answer
to the *Know that I exist!* of all existing things.


3.

If, says the Dahomeyan devil,
someone has courage to enter the fire
the young man will be restored to life.

If, the girl whispers,
I do not go into the fire
I will not be able to live with my soul.

(Her face calm and dark as amber
under the dyed butterfly turban
her back scarified in ostrich-skin patterns.)
        •

4.

Crusaders' wind glinting
off linked scales of sea
ripping the ghostflags
galloping at the fortress
Acre, bloodcaked, lionhearted
raw vomit curdling in the sun
gray walkers walking
straying with a curbed intentness
in and out the inclosures
the gallows, the photographs
of dead Jewish terrorists, aged 15
their fading faces wide-eyed
and out in the crusading sunlight
gray strayers still straying
dusty paths
the mad who live in the dried-up moat
of the War Museum

what are we coming to
what wants these things of us
who wants them


5.

The strain of being born
          over and over has torn your smile into pieces
Often I have seen it broken
          and then re-membered
and wondered how a beauty
          so anarch, so ungelded
will be cared for in this world.
          I want to hand you this
leaflet streaming with rain or tears
          but the words coming clear
something you might find crushed into your hand
          after passing a barricade
               •

and stuff in your raincoat pocket.
    I want this to reach you
who told me once that poetry is nothing sacred
    —no more sacred that is
than other things in your life—
    to answer yes, if life is uncorrupted
no better poetry is wanted.
    I want this to be yours
in the sense that if you find and read it
    it will be there in you already
and the leaflet then merely something
    to leave behind, a little leaf
in the drawer of a sublet room.
    What else does it come down to
but handing on scraps of paper
    little figurines or phials
no stronger than the dry clay they are baked in
    yet more than dry clay or paper
because the imagination crouches in them.
    If we needed fire to remind us
that all true images
    were scooped out of the mud
where our bodies curse and flounder
    then perhaps that fire is coming
to sponge away the scribes and time-servers
    and much that you would have loved will be lost as well
before you could handle it and know it
    just as we almost miss each other
in the ill cloud of mistrust, who might have touched
    hands quickly, shared food or given blood
for each other. I am thinking how we can use what we have
    to invent what we need.

*Winter–Spring* 1968

# *from* Ghazals: Homage to Ghalib

7/12/68

*—for Sheila Rotner*

The clouds are electric in this university.
The lovers astride the tractor burn fissures through the hay.

When I look at that wall I shall think of you
and of what you did not paint there.

Only the truth makes the pain of lifting a hand worthwhile:
the prism staggering under the blows of the raga.

The vanishing-point is the point where he appears.
Two parallel tracks converge, yet there has been no wreck.

To mutilate privacy with a single foolish syllable
is to throw away the search for the one necessary word.

When you read these lines, think of me
and of what I have not written here.


7/14/68: i

In Central Park we talked of our own cowardice.
How many times a day, in this city, are those words spoken?

The tears of the universe aren't all stars, Danton;
some are satellites of brushed aluminum and stainless steel.

He, who was temporary, has joined eternity;
he has deserted us, gone over to the other side.
        •

In the Theatre of the Dust no actor becomes famous.
In the last scene they all are blown away like dust.

"It may be if I had known them I would have loved them."
You were American, Whitman, and those words are yours.

7/14/68: ii

Did you think I was talking about my life?
I was trying to drive a tradition up against the wall.

The field they burned over is greener than all the rest.
You have to watch it, he said, the sparks can travel the roots.

Shot back into this earth's atmosphere
our children's children may photograph these stones.

In the red wash of the darkroom, I see myself clearly;
when the print is developed and handed about, the face
                                        is nothing to me.

For us the work undoes itself over and over:
the grass grows back, the dust collects, the scar breaks open.

7/16/68: i

Blacked-out on a wagon, part of my life cut out forever—
five green hours and forty violet minutes.

A cold spring slowed our lilacs, till a surf broke
violet/white, tender and sensual, misread it if you dare.

I tell you, truth is, at the moment, here
burning outward through our skins.

Eternity streams through my body:
touch it with your hand and see.
        •

Till the walls of the tunnel cave in
and the black river walks on our faces.

7/16/68: ii

When they mow the fields, I see the world reformed
as if by snow, or fire, or physical desire.

First snow. Death of the city. Ghosts in the air.
Your shade among the shadows, interviewing the mist.

The mail came every day, but letters were missing;
by this I knew things were not what they ought to be.

The trees in the long park blurring back
into Olmsted's original dream-work.

The impartial scholar writes me from under house arrest.
I hope you are rotting in hell, Montaigne you bastard.

7/26/68: i

Last night you wrote on the wall: Revolution is poetry.
Today you needn't write; the wall has tumbled down.

We were taught to respect the appearance behind the reality.
Our senses were out on parole, under surveillance.

A pair of eyes imprisoned for years inside my skull
is burning its way outward, the headaches are terrible.

I'm walking through a rubble of broken sculpture, stumbling
here on the spine of a friend, there on the hand of a brother.

All those joinings! and yet we fought so hard to be unique.
Neither alone, nor in anyone's arms, will we end up sleeping.
            •

8/1/68

The order of the small town on the riverbank,
forever at war with the order of the dark and starlit soul.

Were you free then all along, Jim, free at last,
of everything but the white boy's fantasies?

We pleaded guilty till we saw what rectitude was like:
its washed hands, and dead nerve, and sclerotic eye.

I long ago stopped dreaming of pure justice, your honor—
my crime was to believe we could make cruelty obsolete.

The body has been exhumed from the burnt-out bunker;
the teeth counted, the contents of the stomach told over.

And you, Custer, the Squaw-killer, hero of primitive schoolrooms
where are you buried, what is the condition of your bones?

8/4/68

*—for Aijaz Ahmad*

If these are letters, they will have to be misread.
If scribblings on a wall, they must tangle with all the others.

*Fuck reds     Black Power     Angel loves Rosita*
—and a transistor radio answers in Spanish: *Night must fall.*

Prisoners, soldiers, crouching as always, writing,
explaining the unforgivable to a wife, a mother, a lover.

Those faces are blurred and some have turned away
to which I used to address myself so hotly.

How is it, Ghalib, that your grief, resurrected in pieces,
has found its way to this room from your dark house in Delhi?
            •

When they read this poem of mine, they are translators.
Every existence speaks a language of its own.

8/8/68: i

From here on, all of us will be living
like Galileo turning his first tube at the stars.

Obey the little laws and break the great ones
is the preamble to their constitution.

Even to hope is to leap into the unknown,
under the mocking eyes of the way things are.

There's a war on earth, and in the skull, and in the glassy spaces,
between the existing and the non-existing.

I need to live each day through, have them and know them all,
though I can see from here where I'll be standing at the end.

8/8/68: ii

*—for A.H.C.*

A piece of thread ripped-out from a fierce design,
some weaving figured as magic against oppression.

I'm speaking to you as a woman to a man:
when your blood flows I want to hold you in my arms.

How did we get caught up fighting this forest fire,
we, who were only looking for a still place in the woods?

How frail we are, and yet, dispersed, always returning,
the barnacles they keep scraping from the warship's hull.

The hairs on your breast curl so lightly as you lie there,
while the strong heart goes on pounding in its sleep.

From

*The Will to Change*

1971

# November 1968

Stripped
you're beginning to float free
up through the smoke of brushfires
and incinerators
the unleafed branches won't hold you
nor the radar aerials

You're what the autumn knew would happen
after the last collapse
of primary color
once the last absolutes were torn to pieces
you could begin

How you broke open, what sheathed you
until this moment
I know nothing about it
my ignorance of you amazes me
now that I watch you
starting to give yourself away
to the wind

1968

# Study of History

Out there.    The mind of the river
as it might be you.

Lights      blotted by unseen hulls
repetitive shapes passing
dull foam crusting the margin
barges sunk below the water-line with silence.
The scow, drudging on.

Lying in the dark, to think of you
and your harsh traffic
gulls pecking your rubbish    natural historians
mourning your lost purity
pleasure cruisers
witlessly careening you

but this
after all
is the narrows and after
all we have never entirely
known what was done to you upstream
what powers trepanned
which of your channels diverted
what rockface leaned to stare
in your upturned
defenseless
face.

1968

# Planetarium

*Thinking of Caroline Herschel (1750–1848)*
*astronomer, sister of William; and others.*

A woman in the shape of a monster
a monster in the shape of a woman
the skies are full of them

a woman      'in the snow
among the Clocks and instruments
or measuring the ground with poles'

in her 98 years to discover
8 comets

she whom the moon ruled
like us
levitating into the night sky
riding the polished lenses

Galaxies of women, there
doing penance for impetuousness
ribs chilled
in those spaces      of the mind

An eye,

          'virile, precise and absolutely certain'
          from the mad webs of Uranusborg

                              encountering the NOVA

every impulse of light exploding
          •

from the core
as life flies out of us

> Tycho whispering at last
> 'Let me not seem to have lived in vain'

What we see, we see
and seeing is changing

the light that shrivels a mountain
and leaves a man alive

Heartbeat of the pulsar
heart sweating through my body

The radio impulse
pouring in from Taurus

> I am bombarded yet     I stand

I have been standing all my life in the
direct path of a battery of signals
the most accurately transmitted most
untranslatable language in the universe
I am a galactic cloud so deep     so invo-
luted that a light wave could take 15
years to travel through me     And has
taken     I am an instrument in the shape
of a woman trying to translate pulsations
into images     for the relief of the body
and the reconstruction of the mind.

1968

# The Burning of Paper Instead of Children

*I was in danger of*
*verbalizing my moral*
*impulses out of existence.*
*—Daniel Berrigan,*
*on trial in Baltimore.*

1. My neighbor, a scientist and art-collector, telephones me in a state of violent emotion. He tells me that my son and his, aged eleven and twelve, have on the last day of school burned a mathematics textbook in the back-yard. He has forbidden my son to come to his house for a week, and has forbidden his own son to leave the house during that time. "The burning of a book," he says, "arouses terrible sensations in me, memories of Hitler; there are few things that upset me so much as the idea of burning a book."

Back there: the library, walled
with green Britannicas
Looking again
in Dürer's *Complete Works*
for MELANCOLIA, the baffled woman

the crocodiles in Herodotus
the Book of the Dead
the *Trial of Jeanne d'Arc,* so blue
I think, It is her color

and they take the book away
because I dream of her too often

love and fear in a house
knowledge of the oppressor
I know it hurts to burn

    •

2. To imagine a time of silence
or few words
a time of chemistry and music

the hollows above your buttocks
traced by my hand
or, *hair is like flesh,* you said

an age of long silence

relief

from this tongue     this slab of limestone
or reinforced concrete
fanatics and traders
dumped on this coast wildgreen clayred
that breathed once
in signals of smoke
sweep of the wind

knowledge of the oppressor
this is the oppressor's language

yet I need it to talk to you

3. *People suffer highly in poverty and it takes dignity and intelligence to
overcome this suffering. Some of the suffering are: a child did not had din-
ner last night: a child steal because he did not have money to buy it: to hear
a mother say she do not have money to buy food for her children and to see
a child without cloth it will make tears in your eyes.*

(the fracture of order
the repair of speech
to overcome this suffering)

4. We lie under the sheet
after making love, speaking
of loneliness
            •

relieved in a book
relived in a book
so on that page
the clot and fissure
of it appears
words of a man
in pain
a naked word
entering the clot
a hand grasping
through bars:

deliverance

What happens between us
has happened for centuries
we know it from literature

still it happens

sexual jealousy
outflung hand
beating bed

dryness of mouth
after panting

there are books that describe all this
and they are useless

You walk into the woods behind a house
there in that country
you find a temple
built eighteen hundred years ago
you enter without knowing
what it is you enter

so it is with us
    •

no one knows what may happen
though the books tell everything

*burn the texts*      said Artaud

5. I am composing on the typewriter late at night, thinking of today. How well
we all spoke. A language is a map of our failures. Frederick Douglass wrote
an English purer than Milton's. People suffer highly in poverty. There are
methods but we do not use them. Joan, who could not read, spoke some peas-
ant form of French. Some of the suffering are: it is hard to tell the truth; this
is America; I cannot touch you now. In America we have only the present
tense. I am in danger. You are in danger. The burning of a book arouses no
sensation in me. I know it hurts to burn. There are flames of napalm in
Catonsville, Maryland. I know it hurts to burn. The typewriter is overheated,
my mouth is burning, I cannot touch you and this is the oppressor's language.

1968

# I Dream I'm the Death of Orpheus

I am walking rapidly through striations of light and dark thrown
      under an arcade.

I am a woman in the prime of life, with certain powers
and those powers severely limited
by authorities whose faces I rarely see.
I am a woman in the prime of life
driving her dead poet in a black Rolls-Royce
through a landscape of twilight and thorns.
A woman with a certain mission
which if obeyed to the letter will leave her intact.
A woman with the nerves of a panther
a woman with contacts among Hell's Angels
            •

a woman feeling the fullness of her powers
at the precise moment when she must not use them
a woman sworn to lucidity
who sees through the mayhem, the smoky fires
of these underground streets
her dead poet learning to walk backward against the wind
on the wrong side of the mirror

1968

# Letters: March 1969

1.

Foreknown. The victor
sees the disaster through and through.
His soles grind rocksalt
from roads of the resistance.
He shoulders through rows
of armored faces
he might have loved and lived among.
The victory carried like a corpse
from town to town
begins to crawl in the casket.
The summer swindled on
from town to town, our train
stopping and broiling on the rails
long enough to let on who we were.
The disaster sat up with us all night
drinking bottled water, eating fruit,
talking of the conditions that prevailed.
Outside along the railroad cut
they were singing for our death.
                •

2.


Hopes sparkle like water in the clean carafe.
How little it takes
to restore composure.
White napkins, a tray
of napoleons and cherry tarts
compliments of the airline
which has flown us out of danger.
They are torturing the journalist we drank with
last night in the lounge
but we can't be sure of that
here overlooking the runway
three hours and twenty minutes into another life.
If this is done for us
(and this is done for us)
if we are well men wearing bandages
for disguise
if we can choose our scene
stay out of earshot
break the roll and pour
from the clean carafe
if we can desert like soldiers
abjure like thieves
we may well purchase new virtues at the gate
of the other world.


3.


"I am up at sunrise
collecting data.
The reservoir burns green.
Darling, the knives they have on this block alone
would amaze you.
When they ask my profession I say
I'm a student of weapons systems.
The notes I'm putting together are purely
                •

of sentimental value
my briefcase is I swear useless
to foreign powers, to the police
I am not given I say
to revealing my sources
to handing round copies
of my dossier for perusal.
The vulnerable go unarmed.
I myself walk the floor
a ruinously expensive Swiss hunting knife
exposed in my brain
eight blades, each one for a distinct purpose,
laid open as on the desk
of an importer or a fence."


4.


Six months back
*send carbons* you said
but this winter's dashed off in pencil
torn off the pad too fast
for those skills. In the dawn taxi
in the kitchen
burning the succotash
the more I love my life the more
I love you. In a time
of fear. In a city
of fears. In a life
without vacations the paisley fades
winter and summer in the sun
but the best time is now.

My sick friend writes: *what's love?*
*This life is nothing, Adrienne!*

Her hands bled onto the sill.
She had that trick of reaching outward,
          •

the pane was smashed but only
the calvinist northwind
spat in from the sea.
She's a shot hero. A dying poet.
Even now, if we went for her—
but they've gone with rags and putty to fix the pane.
She stays in with her mirrors and anger.

I tear up answers
I once gave, postcards
from riot and famine go up on the walls
valentines stuck in the mirror
flame and curl, loyalties dwindle
the bleak light dries our tears
without relief. I keep coming back to you

in my head, but you couldn't know that, and
I have no carbons. Prince of pity,
what eats out of your hand?
the rodent pain, electric
with exhaustion, mazed and shaken?
I'd have sucked the wound in your hand to sleep
but my lips were trembling.
Tell me how to bear myself,
how it's done, the light kiss falling
accurately
on the cracked palm.

1969

# The Stelae

—*for Arnold Rich*

Last night I met you in my sister's house
risen from the dead
showing me your collection

You are almost at the point of giving things away

It's the stelae on the walls I want
that I never saw before

You offer other objects
I have seen time and time again

I think you think you are giving me
something precious

The stelae are so unlike you
swart, indifferent, incised with signs
you have never deciphered

I never knew you had them
I wonder if you are giving them away

1969

# A Valediction Forbidding Mourning

My swirling wants. Your frozen lips.
The grammar turned and attacked me.
Themes, written under duress.
Emptiness of the notations.

They gave me a drug that slowed the healing of wounds.

I want you to see this before I leave:
the experience of repetition as death
the failure of criticism to locate the pain
the poster in the bus that said:
*my bleeding is under control.*

A red plant in a cemetery of plastic wreaths.

A last attempt: the language is a dialect called metaphor.
These images go unglossed: hair, glacier, flashlight.
When I think of a landscape I am thinking of a time.
When I talk of taking a trip I mean forever.
I could say: those mountains have a meaning
but further than that I could not say.

To do something very common, in my own way.

1970

# *from* Shooting Script

Part I 11/69–2/70

1.

We were bound on the wheel of an endless conversation.

Inside this shell, a tide waiting for someone to enter.

A monologue waiting for you to interrupt it.

A man wading into the surf. The dialogue of the rock with the breaker.

The wave changed instantly by the rock; the rock changed by the wave returning over and over.

The dialogue that lasts all night or a whole lifetime.

A conversation of sounds melting constantly into rhythms.

A shell waiting for you to listen.

A tide that ebbs and flows against a deserted continent.

A cycle whose rhythm begins to change the meaning of words.

A wheel of blinding waves of light, the spokes pulsing out from where we hang together in the turning of an endless conversation.

      •

The meaning that searches for its word like a hermit crab.

A monologue that waits for one listener.

An ear filled with one sound only.

A shell penetrated by meaning.

4.

In my imagination I was the pivot of a fresh beginning.

In rafts they came over the sea; on the island they put up those stones by methods we can only guess at.

If the vegetation grows as thick as this, how can we see what they were seeing?

It is all being made clear, with bulldozers, at Angkor Wat.

The verdure was a false mystery; the baring of the stones is no solution for us now.

Defoliation progresses; concrete is poured, sheets of glass hauled overland in huge trucks and at great cost.

Here we never travailed, never took off our shoes to walk the final mile.

Come and look into this cellar-hole; the is the foundling of the woods.

Humans lived here once; it became sacred only when they went away.

&bull;

5.

Of simple choice they are the villagers; their clothes come with
them like red clay roads they have been walking.

The sole of the foot is a map, the palm of the hand a letter,
learned by heart and worn close to the body.

They seemed strange to me, till I began to recall their dialect.

Poking the spade into the dry loam, listening for the tick of
broken pottery, hoarding the brown and black bits in a dented can.

Evenings, at the table, turning the findings out, pushing them
around with a finger, beginning to dream of fitting them together.

Hiding all this work from them, although they might have helped
me.

Going up at night, hiding the tin can in a closet, where the linoleum
lies in shatters on a back shelf.

Sleeping to dream of the unformed, the veil of water pouring over
the wet clay, the rhythms of choice, the lost methods.

Part II 3–7/70

9.
NEWSREEL

This would not be the war we fought in. See, the foliage is
heavier, there were no hills of that size there.

But I find it impossible not to look for actual persons known
to me and not seen since; impossible not to look for myself.
     •

The scenery angers me, I know there is something wrong, the sun
is too high, the grass too trampled, the peasants' faces too broad,
and the main square of the capital had no arcades like those.

Yet the dead look right, and the roofs of the huts, and the crashed
fuselage burning among the ferns.

But this is not the war I came to see, buying my ticket, stumbling
through the darkness, finding my place among the sleepers and
masturbators in the dark.

I thought of seeing the General who cursed us, whose name they
gave to an expressway; I wanted to see the faces of the dead when
they were living.

Once I know they filmed us, back at the camp behind the lines,
taking showers under the trees and showing pictures of our girls.

Somewhere there is a film of the war we fought in, and it must
contain the flares, the souvenirs, the shadows of the netted brush,
the standing in line of the innocent, the hills that were not of
this size.

Somewhere my body goes taut under the deluge, somewhere I am
naked behind the lines, washing my body in the water of that war.

Someone has that war stored up in metal canisters, a memory he
cannot use, somewhere my innocence is proven with my guilt, but
this would not be the war I fought in.

12.

I was looking for a way out of a lifetime's consolations.

We walked in the wholesale district: closed warehouses, windows,
steeped in sun.

•

I said: those cloths are very old. You said: they have lain in
that window a long time.

When the skeletons of the projects shut off the sunset, when the
sense of the Hudson leaves us, when only by loss of light in the east
do I know that I am living in the west.

When I give up being paraphrased, when I let go, when the
beautiful solutions in their crystal flasks have dried up in the sun,
when the lightbulb bursts on lighting, when the dead bulb rattles
like a seed-pod.

Those cloths are very old, they are mummies' cloths, they have lain
in graves, they were not intended to be sold, the tragedy of this
mistake will soon be clear.

Vacillant needles of Manhattan, describing hour & weather; buying
these descriptions at the cost of missing every other point.

13.

We are driven to odd attempts; once it would not have occurred to
me to put out in a boat, not on a night like this.

Still, it was an instrument, and I had pledged myself to try any
instrument that came my way. Never to refuse one from conviction
of incompetence.

A long time I was simply learning to handle the skiff; I had no
special training and my own training was against me.

I had always heard that darkness and water were a threat.

In spite of this, darkness and water helped me to arrive here.

I watched the lights on the shore I had left for a long time; each
one, it seemed to me, was a light I might have lit, in the old days.
&bull;

14.

Whatever it was: the grains of the glacier caked in the boot-cleats;
ashes spilled on white formica.

The death-col viewed through power-glasses; the cube of ice melting
on stainless steel.

Whatever it was, the image that stopped you, the one on which you
came to grief, projecting it over & over on empty walls.

Now to give up the temptations of the projector; to see instead the
web of cracks filtering across the plaster.

To read there the map of the future, the roads radiating from the
initial split, the filaments thrown out from that impasse.

To reread the instructions on your palm; to find there how the
lifeline, broken, keeps its direction.

To read the etched rays of the bullet-hole left years ago in the
glass; to know in every distortion of the light what fracture is.

To put the prism in your pocket, the thin glass lens, the map
of the inner city, the little book with gridded pages.

To pull yourself up by your own roots; to eat the last meal in
your old neighborhood.

From

*Diving into the
Wreck*

1973

# Trying to Talk with a Man

Out in this desert we are testing bombs,
that's why we came here.

Sometimes I feel an underground river
forcing its way between deformed cliffs
an acute angle of understanding
moving itself like a locus of the sun
into this condemned scenery.

What we've had to give up to get here—
whole LP collections, films we starred in
playing in the neighborhoods, bakery windows
full of dry, chocolate-filled Jewish cookies,
the language of love-letters, of suicide notes,
afternoons on the riverbank
pretending to be children

Coming out to this desert
we meant to change the face of
driving among dull green succulents
walking at noon in the ghost town
surrounded by a silence

that sounds like the silence of the place
except that it came with us
and is familiar
and everything we were saying until now
was an effort to blot it out—
coming out here we are up against it

Out here I feel more helpless
with you than without you

    •

You mention the danger
and list the equipment
we talk of people caring for each other
in emergencies—laceration, thirst—
but you look at me like an emergency

Your dry heat feels like power
your eyes are stars of a different magnitude
they reflect lights that spell out: EXIT
when you get up and pace the floor

talking of the danger
as if it were not ourselves
as if we were testing anything else.

1971


# When We Dead Awaken

*—for E.Y.*

Trying to tell you how
the anatomy of the park
through stained panes, the way
guerrillas are advancing
through minefields, the trash
burning endlessly in the dump
to return to heaven like a stain—
everything outside our skins is an image
of this affliction:
stones on my table, carried by hand
from scenes I trusted
souvenirs of what I once described
as happiness
        •

everything outside my skin
speaks of the fault that sends me limping
even the scars of my decisions
even the sunblaze in the mica-vein
even you, fellow-creature, sister,
sitting across from me, dark with love,
working like me to pick apart
working with me to remake
this trailing knitted thing, this cloth of darkness,
this woman's garment, trying to save the skein.


2.


The fact of being separate
enters your livelihood like a piece of furniture
—a chest of seventeenth-century wood
from somewhere in the North.
It has a huge lock shaped like a woman's head
but the key has not been found.
In the compartments are other keys
to lost doors, an eye of glass.
Slowly you begin to add
things of your own.
You come and go reflected in its panels.
You give up keeping track of anniversaries,
you begin to write in your diaries
more honestly than ever.


3.


The lovely landscape of southern Ohio
betrayed by strip mining, the
thick gold band on the adulterer's finger
the blurred programs of the offshore pirate station
are causes for hesitation.
Here in the matrix of need and anger, the
disproof of what we thought possible
        •

failures of medication
doubts of another's existence
—tell it over and over, the words
get thick with unmeaning—
yet never have we been closer to the truth
of the lies we were living, listen to me:
the faithfulness I can imagine would be a weed
flowering in tar, a blue energy piercing
the massed atoms of a bedrock disbelief.

1971


# From the Prison House

Underneath my lids another eye has opened
it looks nakedly
at the light

that soaks in from the world of pain
even when I sleep

Steadily it regards
everything I am going through

and more

it sees the clubs and rifle-butts
rising and falling
it sees

detail not on TV

the fingers of the policewoman
searching the cunt of the young prostitute
it sees
     •

the roaches dropping into the pan
where they cook the pork
in the House of D

it sees
the violence
embedded in silence

This eye
is not for weeping
its vision
must be unblurred
though tears are on my face

its intent is clarity
it must forget
nothing

1971

# The Mirror in Which Two Are Seen as One

1.

She is the one you call sister.
Her simplest act has glamor,
as when she scales a fish the knife
flashes in her long fingers
no motion wasted or when
rapidly talking of love
she steel-wool burnishes
the battered kettle

&bull;

Love apples cramp you sideways
with sudden emptiness
the cereals glutting you, the grains
ripe clusters picked by hand
Love: the refrigerator
with open door
the ripe steaks bleeding
their hearts out in plastic film
the whipped butter, the apricots
the sour leftovers

A crate is waiting in the orchard
for you to fill it
your hands are raw with scraping
the sharp bark, the thorns
of this succulent tree
Pick, pick, pick
this harvest is a failure
the juice runs down your cheekbones
like sweat or tears


2.


She is the one you call sister
you blaze like lightning about the room
flicker around her like fire
dazzle yourself in her wide eyes
listing her unfelt needs
thrusting the tenets of your life
into her hands

She moves through a world of India print
her body dappled
with softness, the paisley swells at her hip

walking the street in her cotton shift
                •

buying fresh figs because you love them
photographing the ghetto because you took her there

Why are you crying dry up your tears
we are sisters
words fail you in the stare of her hunger
you hand her another book
scored by your pencil
you hand her a record
of two flutes in India reciting


3.


Late summer night the insects
fry in the yellowed lightglobe
your skin burns gold in its light
In this mirror, who are you? Dreams of the nunnery
with its discipline, the nursery
with its nurse, the hospital
where all the powerful ones are masked
the graveyard where you sit on the graves
of women who died in childbirth
and women who died at birth
Dreams of your sister's birth
your mother dying in childbirth over and over
not knowing how to stop
bearing you over and over

your mother dead and you unborn
your two hands grasping your head
drawing it down against the blade of life
your nerves the nerves of a midwife
learning her trade

1971

# Dialogue

She sits with one hand poised against her head, the
other turning an old ring to the light
for hours our talk has beaten
like rain against the screens
a sense of August and heat-lightning
I get up, go to make tea, come back
we look at each other
then she says (and this is what I live through
over and over)—she says: *I do not know
if sex is an illusion*

*I do not know
who I was when I did those things
or who I said I was
or whether I willed to feel
what I had read about
or who in fact was there with me
or whether I knew, even then
that there was doubt about these things*

1972

# Diving into the Wreck

First having read the book of myths,
and loaded the camera,
and checked the edge of the knife-blade,
I put on
the body-armor of black rubber
the absurd flippers
the grave and awkward mask.
I am having to do this
not like Cousteau with his
assiduous team
aboard the sun-flooded schooner
but here alone.

There is a ladder.
The ladder is always there
hanging innocently
close to the side of the schooner.
We know what it is for,
we who have used it.
Otherwise
it's a piece of maritime floss
some sundry equipment.

I go down.
Rung after rung and still
the oxygen immerses me
the blue light
the clear atoms
of our human air.
I go down.
My flippers cripple me,
I crawl like an insect down the ladder
and there is no one
to tell me when the ocean
will begin.

First the air is blue and then
it is bluer and then green and then
black I am blacking out and yet
my mask is powerful
it pumps my blood with power
the sea is another story
the sea is not a question of power
I have to learn alone
to turn my body without force
in the deep element.

And now: it is easy to forget
what I came for
among so many who have always
lived here
swaying their crenellated fans
between the reefs
and besides
you breathe differently down here.

I came to explore the wreck.
The words are purposes.
The words are maps.
I came to see the damage that was done
and the treasures that prevail.
I stroke the beam of my lamp
slowly along the flank
of something more permanent
than fish or weed

the thing I came for:
the wreck and not the story of the wreck
the thing itself and not the myth
the drowned face always staring
toward the sun
the evidence of damage
worn by salt and sway into this threadbare beauty
                .

the ribs of the disaster
curving their assertion
among the tentative haunters.

This is the place.
And I am here, the mermaid whose dark hair
streams black, the merman in his armored body
We circle silently
about the wreck
we dive into the hold.
I am she: I am he

whose drowned face sleeps with open eyes
whose breasts still bear the stress
whose silver, copper, vermeil cargo lies
obscurely inside barrels
half-wedged and left to rot
we are the half-destroyed instruments
that once held to a course
the water-eaten log
the fouled compass

We are, I am, you are
by cowardice or courage
the one who find our way
back to this scene
carrying a knife, a camera
a book of myths
in which
our names do not appear.

1972

# Song

You're wondering if I'm lonely:
OK then, yes, I'm lonely
as a plane rides lonely and level
on its radio beam, aiming
across the Rockies
for the blue-strung aisles
of an airfield on the ocean

You want to ask, am I lonely?
Well, of course, lonely
as a woman driving across country
day after day, leaving behind
mile after mile
little towns she might have stopped
and lived and died in, lonely

If I'm lonely
it must be the loneliness
of waking first, of breathing
dawn's first cold breath on the city
of being the one awake
in a house wrapped in sleep

If I'm lonely
it's with the rowboat ice-fast on the shore
in the last red light of the year
that knows what it is, that knows it's neither
ice nor mud nor winter light
but wood, with a gift for burning

1971

# The Ninth Symphony of Beethoven
# Understood at Last as a Sexual Message

A man in terror of impotence
or infertility, not knowing the difference
a man trying to tell something
howling from the climacteric
music of the entirely
isolated soul
yelling at Joy from the tunnel of the ego
music without the ghost
of another person in it, music
trying to tell something the man
does not want out, would keep if he could
gagged and bound and flogged with chords of Joy
where everything is silence and the
beating of a bloody fist upon
a splintered table

1972

# Rape

There is a cop who is both prowler and father:
he comes from your block, grew up with your brothers,
had certain ideals.
You hardly know him in his boots and silver badge,
on horseback, one hand touching his gun.
        •

You hardly know him but you have to get to know him:
he has access to machinery that could kill you.
He and his stallion clop like warlords among the trash,
his ideals stand in the air, a frozen cloud
from between his unsmiling lips.

And so, when the time comes, you have to turn to him,
the maniac's sperm still greasing your thighs,
your mind whirling like crazy. You have to confess
to him, you are guilty of the crime
of having been forced.

And you see his blue eyes, the blue eyes of all the family
whom you used to know, grow narrow and glisten,
his hand types out the details
and he wants them all
but the hysteria in your voice pleases him best.

You hardly know him but now he thinks he knows you:
he has taken down your worst moment
on a machine and filed it in a file.
He knows, or thinks he knows, how much you imagined;
he knows, or thinks he knows, what you secretly wanted.

He has access to machinery that could get you put away;
and if, in the sickening light of the precinct,
and if, in the sickening light of the precinct,
your details sound like a portrait of your confessor,
will you swallow, will you deny them, will you lie your way home?

1972

# Burning Oneself In

In a bookstore on the East Side
I read a veteran's testimony:

the running down, for no reason,
of an old woman in South Vietnam
by a U.S. Army truck

The heat-wave is over
Lifeless, sunny, the East Side
rests under its awnings

Another summer
The flames go on feeding

and a dull heat permeates the ground
of the mind, the burn has settled in
as if it had no more question

of its right to go on devouring
the rest of a lifetime,
the rest of history

Pieces of information, like this one
blow onto the heap

they keep it fed, whether we will it or not,
another summer, and another
of suffering quietly

in bookstores, in the parks
however we may scream we are
suffering quietly

1972

# From a Survivor

The pact that we made was the ordinary pact
of men & women in those days

I don't know who we thought we were
that our personalities
could resist the failures of the race

Lucky or unlucky, we didn't know
the race had failures of that order
and that we were going to share them

Like everybody else, we thought of ourselves as special

Your body is as vivid to me
as it ever was: even more

since my feeling for it is clearer:
I know what it could and could not do

it is no longer
the body of a god
or anything with power over my life

Next year it would have been 20 years
and you are wastefully dead
who might have made the leap
we talked, too late, of making

which I live now
not as a leap
but a succession of brief, amazing movements

each one making possible the next

1972

# August

Two horses in yellow light
eating windfall apples under a tree

as summer tears apart     milkweeds stagger
and grasses grow more ragged

They say there are ions in the sun
neutralizing magnetic fields on earth

Some way to explain
what this week has been, and the one before it!

If I am flesh sunning on rock
if I am brain burning in fluorescent light

if I am dream like a wire with fire
throbbing along it

if I am death to man
I have to know it

His mind is too simple, I cannot go on
sharing his nightmares

My own are becoming clearer, they open
into prehistory

which looks like a village lit with blood
where all the fathers are crying: *My son is mine!*

1972

# Uncollected Poems

1950–1974

# The Prisoners

Enclosed in this disturbing mutual wood,
Wounded alike by thorns of the same tree,
We seek in hopeless war each others' blood
Though suffering in one identity.
Each to the other prey and huntsman known,
Still driven together, lonelier than alone.

Strange mating of the loser and the lost!
With faces stiff as mourners', we intrude
Forever on the one each turns from most,
Each wandering in a double solitude.
The unpurged ghosts of passion bound by pride
Who wake in isolation, side by side.

1950


# At the Jewish New Year

For more than five thousand years
This calm September day
With yellow in the leaf
Has lain in the kernel of Time
While the world outside the walls
Has had its turbulent say
And history like a long
Snake has crawled on its way
And is crawling onward still.
And we have little to tell
•

On this or any feast
Except of the terrible past.
Five thousand years are cast
Down before the wondering child
Who must expiate them all.

Some of us have replied
In the bitterness of youth
Or the qualms of middle-age:
"If Time is unsatisfied,
And all our fathers have suffered
Can never be enough,
Why, then, we choose to forget.
Let our forgetting begin
With those age-old arguments
In which their minds were wound
Like musty phylacteries;
And we choose to forget as well
Those cherished histories
That made our old men fond,
And already are strange to us.

"Or let us, being today
Too rational to cry out,
Or trample underfoot
What after all preserves
A certain savor yet—
Though torn up by the roots—
Let us make our compromise
With the terror and the guilt
And view as curious relics
Once found in daily use
The mythology, the names
That, however Time has corrupted
Their ancient purity
Still burn like yellow flames,
But their fire is not for us."

.

And yet, however we choose
To deny or to remember,
Though on the calendars
We wake and suffer by,
This day is merely one
Of thirty in September—
In the kernel of the mind
The new year must renew
This day, as for our kind
Over five thousand years,
The task of being ourselves.
Whatever we strain to forget,
Our memory must be long.

May the taste of honey linger
Under the bitterest tongue.

1955

# Dien Bien Phu

A nurse on the battlefield
wounded herself, but working

    dreams
        that each man she touches
        is a human grenade
                an anti-personnel weapon
                that can explode in her arms

    How long
        can she go on like this
        putting mercy
        ahead of survival
    •

She is walking
in a white dress stained
with earth and blood

          down a road lined
          with fields long
          given up       blasted

     cemeteries of one name
     or two

A hand
juts out like barbed wire
it is terribly alone

if she takes it
          will it slash her wrists again

if she passes it by

          will she turn into a case
          of shell-shock, eyes
          glazed forever on the

                blank chart of
                amnesia

1973

# Re-forming the Crystal

I am trying to imagine
how it feels to you
to want a woman
  •

trying to hallucinate
desire
centered in a cock
focused like a burning-glass

desire without discrimination:
to want a woman like a fix

Desire: yes: the sudden knowledge, like coming out of 'flu, that the body is sexual. Walking in the streets with that knowledge. That evening in the plane from Pittsburgh, fantasizing going to meet you. Walking through the airport blazing with energy and joy. But knowing all along that you were not the source of that energy and joy; you were a man, a stranger, a name, a voice on the telephone, a friend; this desire was mine, this energy my energy; it could be used a hundred ways, and going to meet you could be one of them.

Tonight is a different kind of night.
I sit in the car, racing the engine,
calculating the thinness of the ice.
In my head I am already threading the beltways
that rim this city,
all the old roads that used to wander the country
having been lost.
Tonight I understand
my photo on the license is not me,
my
name on the marriage-contract was not mine.
If I remind you of my father's favorite daughter,
look again. The woman
I needed to call my mother
was silenced before I was born.

Tonight if the battery charges I want to take the car out on sheet-ice; I want to understand my fear both of the machine and of the accidents of nature. My desire for you is not trivial; I can compare it with the greatest of those accidents. But the energy it draws on might lead to racing a cold engine, cracking the frozen spiderweb,

•

parachuting into the field of a poem wired with danger, or to a trip through gorges and canyons, into the cratered night of female memory, where delicately and with intense care the chieftainess inscribes upon the ribs of the volcano the name of the one she has chosen.

1973

# White Night

Light at a window. Someone up
at this snail-still hour.
We who work this way have often worked
in solitude. I've had to guess at her
sewing her skin together as I sew mine
though
with a different
stitch.

Dawn after dawn, this neighbor
burns like a candle
dragging her bedspread through the dark house
to her dark bed
her head
full of runes, syllables, refrains,
this accurate dreamer

sleepwalks the kitchen
like a white moth,
an elephant, a guilt.
Somebody tried to put her
to rest under an afghan
knitted with wools the color of grass and blood

　　　　•

but she has risen. Her lamplight
licks at the icy panes
and melts into the dawn.
They will never prevent her
who sleep the stone sleep of the past,
the sleep of the drugged.
One crystal second, I flash

an eye across the cold
unwrapping of light between us
into her darkness-lancing eye
—that's all. Dawn is the test, the agony
but we were meant to see it:
After this, we may sleep, my sister,
while the flames rise higher and higher, we can sleep.

1974

# From an Old House in America

1.

Deliberately, long ago
the carcasses

of old bugs crumbled
into the rut of the window

and we started sleeping here
Fresh June bugs batter this June's

screens, June-lightning batters
the spiderweb
•

I sweep the wood-dust
from the wood-box

the snout of the vacuum cleaner
sucks the past away

2.

Other lives were lived here:
mostly un-articulate

yet someone left her creamy signature
in the trail of rusticated

narcissus straggling up
through meadowgrass and vetch

Families breathed close
boxed-in from the cold

hard times, short growing season
the old rainwater cistern

hulks in the cellar

3.

Like turning through the contents of a drawer:
these rusted screws, this empty vial

useless, this box of watercolor paints
dried to insolubility—

but this—
this pack of cards with no card missing

still playable
and three good fuses

•

and this toy: a little truck
scarred red, yet all its wheels still turn

The humble tenacity of things
waiting for people, waiting for months, for years


4.

*Often rebuked, yet always back returning*
I place my hand on the hand

of the dead, invisible palm-print
on the doorframe

spiked with daylilies, green leaves
catching in the screen door

or I read the backs of old postcards
curling from thumbtacks, winter and summer

fading through cobweb-tinted panes—
white church in Norway

Dutch hyacinths bleeding azure
red beach on Corsica

set-pieces of the world
stuck to this house of plank

I flash on wife and husband
embattled, in the years

that dried, dim ink was wet
those signatures

•

5.

If they call me man-hater, you
would have known it for a lie

but the *you* I want to speak to
has become your death

If I dream of you these days
I know my dreams are mine and not of you

yet something hangs between us
older and stranger than ourselves

like a translucent curtain, a sheet of water
a dusty window

the irreducible, incomplete connection
between the dead and living

or between man and woman in this
savagely fathered and unmothered world

6.

The other side of a translucent
curtain, a sheet of water

a dusty window, Non-being
utters its flat tones

the speech of an actor learning his lines
phonetically

the final autistic statement
of the self-destroyer

•

All my energy reaches out tonight
to comprehend a miracle beyond

raising the dead: the undead to watch
back on the road of birth

7.

I am an American woman:
I turn that over

like a leaf pressed in a book
I stop and look up from

into the coals of the stove
or the black square of the window

Foot-slogging through the Bering Strait
jumping from the *Arbella* to my death

chained to the corpse beside me
I feel my pains begin

I am washed up on this continent
shipped here to be fruitful

my body a hollow ship
bearing sons to the wilderness

sons who ride away
on horseback, daughters

whose juices drain like mine
into the *arroyo* of stillbirths, massacres

Hanged as witches, sold as breeding-wenches
my sisters leave me
            •

I am not the wheatfield
nor the virgin forest

I never chose this place
yet I am of it now

In my decent collar, in the daguerreotype
I pierce its legend with my look

my hands wring the necks of prairie chickens
I am used to blood

When the men hit the hobo track
I stay on with the children

my power is brief and local
but I know my power

I have lived in isolation
from other women, so much

in the mining camps, the first cities
the Great Plains winters

Most of the time, in my sex, I was alone

8.

Tonight in this northeast kingdom
striated iris stand in a jar with daisies

the porcupine gnaws in the shed
fireflies beat and simmer

caterpillars begin again
their long, innocent climb
                •

the length of leaves of burdock
or webbing of a garden chair

plain and ordinary things
speak softly

the light square on old wallpaper
where a poster has fallen down

Robert Indiana's LOVE
leftover of a decade

9.

I do not want to simplify
Or: I would simplify

by naming the complexity
It was made over-simple all along

the separation of powers
the allotment of sufferings

her spine cracking in labor
his plow driving across the Indian graves

her hand unconscious on the cradle, her mind
with the wild geese

his mother-hatred driving him
into exile from the earth

the refugee couple with their cardboard luggage
standing on the ramshackle landing-stage

he with fingers frozen around his Law
she with her down quilt sewn through iron nights
        •

—the weight of the old world, plucked
drags after them, a random feather-bed

10.

Her children dead of diphtheria, she
set herself on fire with kerosene

(O Lord I was unworthy
Thou didst find me out)

she left the kitchen scrubbed
down to the marrow of its boards

"The penalty for barrenness
is emptiness

my punishment is my crime
what I have failed to do, is me . . ."

—Another month without a show
and this the seventh year

*O Father let this thing pass out of me*
*I swear to You*

*I will live for the others, asking nothing*
*I will ask nothing, ever, for myself*

11.

Out back of this old house
*datura* tangles with a gentler weed

its spiked pods smelling
of bad dreams and death
                •

I reach through the dark, groping
past spines of nightmare

to brush the leaves of sensuality
A dream of tenderness

wrestles with all I know of history
I cannot now lie down

with a man who fears my power
or reaches for me as for death

or with a lover who imagines
we are not in danger

12.

If it was lust that had defined us—
their lust and fear of our deep places

we have done our time
as faceless torsos licked by fire

we are in the open, on our way—
our counterparts

the pinyon jay, the small
gilt-winged insect

the Cessna throbbing level
the raven floating in the gorge

the rose and violet vulva of the earth
filling with darkness

yet deep within a single sparkle
of red, a human fire

•

and near and yet above the western planet
calmly biding her time


13.


They were the distractions, lust and fear
but are

themselves a key
Everything that can be used, will be:

the fathers in their ceremonies
the genital contests

the cleansing of blood from pubic hair
the placenta buried and guarded

their terror of blinding
by the look of her who bore them

If you do not believe
that fear and hatred

read the lesson again
in the old dialect


14.


*But can't you see me as a human being*
he said

*What is a human being*
she said

*I try to understand*
he said

•

*what will you undertake*
she said

*will you punish me for history*
he said

*what will you undertake*
she said

*do you believe in collective guilt*
he said

*let me look in your eyes*
she said

15.

Who is here. The Erinyes.
One to sit in judgment.

One to speak tenderness.
One to inscribe the verdict on the canyon wall.

If you have not confessed
the damage

if you have not recognized
the Mother of reparations

if you have not come to terms
with the women in the mirror

if you have not come to terms
with the inscription

the terms of the ordeal
the discipline     the verdict
          •

if still you are on your way
still She awaits your coming

16.

"Such women are dangerous
to the order of things"

and yes, we will be dangerous
to ourselves

groping through spines of nightmare
(*datura* tangling with a simpler herb)

because the line dividing
lucidity from darkness

is yet to be marked out

Isolation, the dream
of the frontier woman

leveling her rifle along
the homestead fence

still snares our pride
—a suicidal leaf

laid under the burning-glass
in the sun's eye

Any woman's death diminishes me

1974

# The Fact of a Doorframe

means there is something to hold
onto with both hands
while slowly thrusting my forehead against the wood
and taking it away
one of the oldest motions of suffering
as Makeba sings
a courage-song for warriors
music is suffering made powerful

I think of the story
of the goose-girl who passed through the high gate
where the head of her favorite mare
was nailed to the arch
and in a human voice
*If she could see thee now, thy mother's heart would break*
said the head
of Falada

Now, again, poetry,
violent, arcane, common,
hewn of the commonest living substance
into archway, portal, frame
I grasp for you, your bloodstained splinters, your
ancient and stubborn poise
—as the earth trembles—
burning out from the grain

1974

From

# *The Dream of a Common Language*

1978

# Power

Living    in the earth-deposits    of our history

Today a backhoe divulged      out of a crumbling flank of earth
one bottle    amber    perfect    a hundred-year-old
cure for fever    or melancholy    a tonic
for living on this earth      in the winters of this climate

Today I was reading about Marie Curie:
she must have known she suffered    from radiation sickness
her body bombarded for years      by the element
she had purified
It seems she denied to the end
the source of the cataracts on her eyes
the cracked and suppurating skin    of her finger-ends
till she could no longer hold    a test-tube or a pencil

She died    a famous woman    denying
her wounds
denying
her wounds    came    from the same source as her power

1974

# Hunger

*—for Audre Lorde*

1.

A fogged hill-scene on an enormous continent,
intimacy rigged with terrors,
a sequence of blurs the Chinese painter's ink-stick planned,
a scene of desolation comforted
by two human figures recklessly exposed,
leaning together in a sticklike boat
in the foreground. Maybe we look like this,
I don't know. I'm wondering
whether we even have what we think we have—
lighted windows signifying shelter,
a film of domesticity
over fragile roofs. I know I'm partly somewhere else—
huts strung across a drought-stretched land
not mine, dried breasts, mine and not mine, a mother
watching my children shrink with hunger.
I live in my Western skin,
my Western vision, torn
and flung to what I can't control or even fathom.
Quantify suffering, you could rule the world.

2.

They cán rule the world while they can persuade us
our pain belongs in some order.
Is death by famine worse than death by suicide,
than a life of famine and suicide, if a black lesbian dies,
if a white prostitute dies, if a woman genius
            •

starves herself to feed others,
self-hatred battening on her body?
Something that kills us or leaves us half-alive
is raging under the name of an "act of god"
in Chad, in Niger, in the Upper Volta—
yes, that male god that acts on us and on our children,
that male State that acts on us and on our children
till our brains are blunted by malnutrition,
yet sharpened by the passion for survival,
our powers expended daily on the struggle
to hand a kind of life on to our children,
to change reality for our lovers
even in a single trembling drop of water.

3.

We can look at each other through both our lifetimes
like those two figures in the sticklike boat
flung together in the Chinese ink-scene;
even our intimacies are rigged with terror.
Quantify suffering? My guilt at least is open,
I stand convicted by all my convictions—
you, too. We shrink from touching
our power, we shrink away, we starve ourselves
and each other, we're scared shitless
of what it could be to take and use our love,
hose it on a city, on a world,
to wield and guide its spray, destroying
poisons, parasites, rats, viruses—
like the terrible mothers we long and dread to be.

4.

The decision to feed the world
is the real decision. No revolution
has chosen it. For that choice requires
that women shall be free.
        •

I choke on the taste of bread in North America
but the taste of hunger in North America
is poisoning me. Yes, I'm alive to write these words,
to leaf through Kollwitz's women
huddling the stricken children into their stricken arms
the "mothers" drained of milk, the "survivors" driven
to self-abortion, self-starvation, to a vision
bitter, concrete, and wordless.
I'm alive to want more than life,
want it for others starving and unborn,
to name the deprivations boring
into my will, my affections, into the brains
of daughters, sisters, lovers caught in the crossfire
of terrorists of the mind.
In the black mirror of the subway window
hangs my own face, hollow with anger and desire.
Swathed in exhaustion, on the trampled newsprint,
a woman shields a dead child from the camera.
The passion to be inscribes her body.
Until we find each other, we are alone.


1974–1975


# Cartographies of Silence

1.

A conversation begins
with a lie. And each

speaker of the so-called common language feels
the ice-floe split, the drift apart

•

as if powerless, as if up against
a force of nature

A poem can begin
with a lie. And be torn up.

A conversation has other laws
recharges itself with its own

false energy. Cannot be torn
up. Infiltrates our blood. Repeats itself.

Inscribes with its unreturning stylus
the isolation it denies.

2.

The classical music station
playing hour upon hour in the apartment

the picking up and picking up
and again picking up the telephone

The syllables uttering
the old script over and over

The loneliness of the liar
living in the formal network of the lie

twisting the dials to drown the terror
beneath the unsaid word

3.

The technology of silence
The rituals, etiquette
&bull;

the blurring of terms
silence not absence

of words or music or even
raw sounds

Silence can be a plan
rigorously executed

the blueprint to a life

It is a presence
it has a history     a form

Do not confuse it
with any kind of absence

4.

How calm, how inoffensive these words
begin to seem to me

though begun in grief and anger
Can I break through this film of the abstract

without wounding myself or you
there is enough pain here

This is why the classical or the jazz music station plays?
to give a ground of meaning to our pain?

5.

The silence that strips bare:
In Dreyer's *Passion of Joan*
    •

Falconetti's face, hair shorn, a great geography
mutely surveyed by the camera

If there were a poetry where this could happen
not as blank spaces or as words

stretched like a skin over meanings
but as silence falls at the end

of a night through which two people
have talked till dawn

6.

The scream
of an illegitimate voice

It has ceased to hear itself, therefore
it asks itself

How dó I exist?

This was the silence I wanted to break in you
I had questions but you would not answer

I had answers but you could not use them
This is useless to you and perhaps to others

7.

It was an old theme even for me:
Language cannot do everything—

chalk it on the walls where the dead poets
lie in their mausoleums

•

If at the will of the poet the poem
could turn into a thing

a granite flank laid bare, a lifted head
alight with dew

If it could simply look you in the face
with naked eyeballs, not letting you turn

till you, and I who long to make this thing,
were finally clarified together in its stare

8.

No. Let me have this dust,
these pale clouds dourly lingering, these words

moving with ferocious accuracy
like the blind child's fingers

or the newborn infant's mouth
violent with hunger

No one can give me, I have long ago
taken this method

whether of bran pouring from the loose-woven sack
or of the bunsen-flame turned low and blue

If from time to time I envy
the pure annunciations to the eye

the *visio beatifica*
if from time to time I long to turn

like the Eleusinian hierophant
holding up a simple ear of grain

•

for return to the concrete and everlasting world
what in fact I keep choosing

are these words, these whispers, conversations
from which time after time the truth breaks moist and green.

1975

# Twenty-One Love Poems

### I

Wherever in this city, screens flicker
with pornography, with science-fiction vampires,
victimized hirelings bending to the lash,
we also have to walk . . . if simply as we walk
through the rainsoaked garbage, the tabloid cruelties
of our own neighborhoods.
We need to grasp our lives inseparable
from those rancid dreams, that blurt of metal, those disgraces,
and the red begonia perilously flashing
from a tenement sill six stories high,
or the long-legged young girls playing ball
in the junior highschool playground.
No one has imagined us. We want to live like trees,
sycamores blazing through the sulfuric air,
dappled with scars, still exuberantly budding,
our animal passion rooted in the city.

### II

I wake up in your bed. I know I have been dreaming.
Much earlier, the alarm broke us from each other,
        •

you've been at your desk for hours. I know what I dreamed:
our friend the poet comes into my room
where I've been writing for days,
drafts, carbons, poems are scattered everywhere,
and I want to show her one poem
which is the poem of my life. But I hesitate,
and wake. You've kissed my hair
to wake me. *I dreamed you were a poem,*
I say, *a poem I wanted to show someone . . .*
and I laugh and fall dreaming again
of the desire to show you to everyone I love,
to move openly together
in the pull of gravity, which is not simple,
which carries the feathered grass a long way down the upbreathing air.


III

Since we're not young, weeks have to do time
for years of missing each other. Yet only this odd warp
in time tells me we're not young.
Did I ever walk the morning streets at twenty,
my limbs streaming with a purer joy?
did I lean from any window over the city
listening for the future
as I listen here with nerves tuned for your ring?
And you, you move toward me with the same tempo.
Your eyes are everlasting, the green spark
of the blue-eyed grass of early summer,
the green-blue wild cress washed by the spring.
At twenty, yes: we thought we'd live forever.
At forty-five, I want to know even our limits.
I touch you knowing we weren't born tomorrow,
and somehow, each of us will help the other live,
and somewhere, each of us must help the other die.
                •

IV

I come home from you through the early light of spring
flashing off ordinary walls, the Pez Dorado,
the Discount Wares, the shoe-store. . . . I'm lugging my sack
of groceries, I dash for the elevator
where a man, taut, elderly, carefully composed
lets the door almost close on me. —*For god's sake hold it!*
I croak at him. —*Hysterical,*—he breathes my way.
I let myself into the kitchen, unload my bundles,
make coffee, open the window, put on Nina Simone
singing *Here comes the sun.* . . . I open the mail,
drinking delicious coffee, delicious music,
my body still both light and heavy with you. The mail
lets fall a Xerox of something written by a man
aged 27, a hostage, tortured in prison:
*My genitals have been the object of such a sadistic display
they keep me constantly awake with the pain . . .*
*Do whatever you can to survive.*
*You know, I think that men love wars . . .*
And my incurable anger, my unmendable wounds
break open further with tears, I am crying helplessly,
and they still control the world, and you are not in my arms.

V

This apartment full of books could crack open
to the thick jaws, the bulging eyes
of monsters, easily: Once open the books, you have to face
the underside of everything you've loved—
the rack and pincers held in readiness, the gag
even the best voices have had to mumble through,
the silence burying unwanted children—
women, deviants, witnesses—in desert sand.
Kenneth tells me he's been arranging his books
so he can look at Blake and Kafka while he types;
yes; and we still have to reckon with Swift
                •

loathing the woman's flesh while praising her mind,
Goethe's dread of the Mothers, Claudel vilifying Gide,
and the ghosts—their hands clasped for centuries—
of artists dying in childbirth, wise-women charred at the stake,
centuries of books unwritten piled behind these shelves;
and we still have to stare into the absence
of men who would not, women who could not, speak
to our life—this still unexcavated hole
called civilization, this act of translation, this half-world.


VI


Your small hands, precisely equal to my own—
only the thumb is larger, longer—in these hands
I could trust the world, or in many hands like these,
handling power-tools or steering-wheel
or touching a human face. . . . Such hands could turn
the unborn child rightways in the birth canal
or pilot the exploratory rescue-ship
through icebergs, or piece together
the fine, needle-like sherds of a great krater-cup
bearing on its sides
figures of ecstatic women striding
to the sibyl's den or the Eleusinian cave—
such hands might carry out an unavoidable violence
with such restraint, with such a grasp
of the range and limits of violence
that violence ever after would be obsolete.


VII


What kind of beast would turn its life into words?
What atonement is this all about?
—and yet, writing words like these, I'm also living.
Is all this close to the wolverines' howled signals,
that modulated cantata of the wild?
or, when away from you I try to create you in words,
                •

am I simply using you, like a river or a war?
And how have I used rivers, how have I used wars
to escape writing of the worst thing of all—
not the crimes of others, not even our own death,
but the failure to want our freedom passionately enough
so that blighted elms, sick rivers, massacres would seem
mere emblems of that desecration of ourselves?

## VIII

I can see myself years back at Sunion,
hurting with an infected foot, Philoctetes
in woman's form, limping the long path,
lying on a headland over the dark sea,
looking down the red rocks to where a soundless curl
of white told me a wave had struck,
imagining the pull of that water from that height,
knowing deliberate suicide wasn't my métier,
yet all the time nursing, measuring that wound.
Well, that's finished. The woman who cherished
her suffering is dead. I am her descendant.
I love the scar-tissue she handed on to me,
but I want to go on from here with you
fighting the temptation to make a career of pain.

## IX

Your silence today is a pond where drowned things live
I want to see raised dripping and brought into the sun.
It's not my own face I see there, but other faces,
even your face at another age.
Whatever's lost there is needed by both of us—
a watch of old gold, a water-blurred fever chart,
a key. . . . Even the silt and pebbles of the bottom
deserve their glint of recognition. I fear this silence,
this inarticulate life. I'm waiting
for a wind that will gently open this sheeted water
        •

for once, and show me what I can do
for you, who have often made the unnameable
nameable for others, even for me.


X


Your dog, tranquil and innocent, dozes through
our cries, our murmured dawn conspiracies
our telephone calls. She knows—what can she know?
If in my human arrogance I claim to read
her eyes, I find there only my own animal thoughts:
that creatures must find each other for bodily comfort,
that voices of the psyche drive through the flesh
further than the dense brain could have foretold,
that the planetary nights are growing cold for those
on the same journey, who want to touch
one creature-traveler clear to the end;
that without tenderness, we are in hell.


XI


Every peak is a crater. This is the law of volcanoes,
making them eternally and visibly female.
No height without depth, without a burning core,
though our straw soles shred on the hardened lava.
I want to travel with you to every sacred mountain
smoking within like the sibyl stooped over his tripod,
I want to reach for your hand as we scale the path,
to feel your arteries glowing in my clasp,
never failing to note the small, jewel-like flower
unfamiliar to us, nameless till we rename her,
that clings to the slowly altering rock—
that detail outside ourselves that brings us to ourselves,
was here before us, knew we would come, and sees beyond us.
                •

## XII

Sleeping, turning in turn like planets
rotating in their midnight meadow:
a touch is enough to let us know
we're not alone in the universe, even in sleep:
the dream-ghosts of two worlds
walking their ghost-towns, almost address each other.
I've wakened to your muttered words
spoken light- or dark-years away
as if my own voice had spoken.
But we have different voices, even in sleep,
and our bodies, so alike, are yet so different
and the past echoing through our bloodstreams
is freighted with different language, different meanings—
though in any chronicle of the world we share
it could be written with new meaning
we were two lovers of one gender,
we were two women of one generation.

## XIII

The rules break like a thermometer,
quicksilver spills across the charted systems,
we're out in a country that has no language
no laws, we're chasing the raven and the wren
through gorges unexplored since dawn
whatever we do together is pure invention
the maps they gave us were out of date
by years . . . we're driving through the desert
wondering if the water will hold out
the hallucinations turn to simple villages
the music on the radio comes clear—
neither *Rosenkavalier* nor *Götterdämmerung*
but a woman's voice singing old songs
with new words, with a quiet bass, a flute
plucked and fingered by women outside the law.

•

XIV

It was your vision of the pilot
confirmed my vision of you: you said, *He keeps*
*on steering headlong into the waves, on purpose*
while we crouched in the open hatchway
vomiting into plastic bags
for three hours between St. Pierre and Miquelon.
I never felt closer to you.
In the close cabin where the honeymoon couples
huddled in each other's laps and arms
I put my hand on your thigh
to comfort both of us, your hand came over mine,
we stayed that way, suffering together
in our bodies, as if all suffering
were physical, we touched so in the presence
of strangers who knew nothing and cared less
vomiting their private pain
as if all suffering were physical.

*(THE FLOATING POEM, UNNUMBERED)*

Whatever happens with us, your body
will haunt mine—tender, delicate
your lovemaking, like the half-curled frond
of the fiddlehead fern in forests
just washed by sun. Your traveled, generous thighs
between which my whole face has come and come—
the innocence and wisdom of the place my tongue has found there—
the live, insatiate dance of your nipples in my mouth—
your touch on me, firm, protective, searching
me out, your strong tongue and slender fingers
reaching where I had been waiting years for you
in my rose-wet cave—whatever happens, this is.
                    •

XV

If I lay on that beach with you
white, empty, pure green water warmed by the Gulf Stream
and lying on that beach we could not stay
because the wind drove fine sand against us
as if it were against us
if we tried to withstand it and we failed—
if we drove to another place
to sleep in each other's arms
and the beds were narrow like prisoners' cots
and we were tired and did not sleep together
and this was what we found, so this is what we did—
was the failure ours?
If I cling to circumstances I could feel
not responsible. Only she who says
she did not choose, is the loser in the end.

XVI

Across a city from you, I'm with you,
just as an August night
moony, inlet-warm, seabathed, I watched you sleep,
the scrubbed, sheenless wood of the dressing-table
cluttered with our brushes, books, vials in the moonlight—
or a salt-mist orchard, lying at your side
watching red sunset through the screendoor of the cabin,
G minor Mozart on the tape-recorder,
falling asleep to the music of the sea.
This island of Manhattan is wide enough
for both of us, and narrow:
I can hear your breath tonight, I know how your face
lies upturned, the halflight tracing
your generous, delicate mouth
where grief and laughter sleep together.
        •

## XVII

No one's fated or doomed to love anyone.
The accidents happen, we're not heroines,
they happen in our lives like car crashes,
books that change us, neighborhoods
we move into and come to love.
*Tristan und Isolde* is scarcely the story,
women at least should know the difference
between love and death. No poison cup,
no penance. Merely a notion that the tape-recorder
should have caught some ghost of us: that tape-recorder
not merely played but should have listened to us,
and could instruct those after us:
this we were, this is how we tried to love,
and these are the forces they had ranged against us,
and these are the forces we had ranged within us,
within us and against us, against us and within us.

## XVIII

Rain on the West Side Highway,
red light at Riverside:
*the more I live the more I think*
*two people together is a miracle.*
You're telling the story of your life
for once, a tremor breaks the surface of your words.
The story of our lives becomes our lives.
Now you're in fugue across what some I'm sure
Victorian poet called the *salt estranging sea.*
Those are the words that come to mind.
I feel estrangement, yes. As I've felt dawn
pushing toward daybreak. Something: a cleft of light—?
Close between grief and anger, a space opens
where I am Adrienne alone. And growing colder.

•

## XIX

Can it be growing colder when I begin
to touch myself again, adhesions pull away?
When slowly the naked face turns from staring backward
and looks into the present,
the eye of winter, city, anger, poverty, and death
and the lips part and say: *I mean to go on living?*
Am I speaking coldly when I tell you in a dream
or in this poem, *There are no miracles?*
(I told you from the first I wanted daily life,
this island of Manhattan was island enough for me.)
If I could let you know—
two women together is a work
nothing in civilization has made simple,
two people together is a work
heroic in its ordinariness,
the slow-picked, halting traverse of a pitch
where the fiercest attention becomes routine
—look at the faces of those who have chosen it.

## XX

That conversation we were always on the edge
of having, runs on in my head,
at night the Hudson trembles in New Jersey light
polluted water yet reflecting even
sometimes the moon
and I discern a woman
I loved, drowning in secrets, fear wound round her throat
and choking her like hair. And this is she
with whom I tried to speak, whose hurt, expressive head
turning aside from pain, is dragged down deeper
where it cannot hear me,
and soon I shall know I was talking to my own soul.
    •

XXI

The dark lintels, the blue and foreign stones
of the great round rippled by stone implements
the midsummer night light rising from beneath
the horizon—when I said "a cleft of light"
I meant this. And this is not Stonehenge
simply nor any place but the mind
casting back to where her solitude,
shared, could be chosen without loneliness,
not easily nor without pains to stake out
the circle, the heavy shadows, the great light.
I choose to be a figure in that light,
half-blotted by darkness, something moving
across that space, the color of stone
greeting the moon, yet more than stone:
a woman. I choose to walk here. And to draw this circle.

1974–1976


# A Woman Dead in Her Forties

1.

Your breasts/    sliced-off    The scars
dimmed    as they would have to be
years later

All the women I grew up with are sitting
half-naked on rocks    in sun
we look at each other    and
are not ashamed

and you too have taken off your blouse
but this was not what you wanted:
            •

to show your scarred, deleted torso

I barely glance at you
as if my look could scald you
though I'm the one who loved you

I want to touch my fingers
to where your breasts had been
but we never did such things

You hadn't thought everyone
would look so perfect
unmutilated

you pull on
your blouse again:    stern statement:

*There are things I will not share*
*with everyone*


2.


You send me back to share
my own scars    first of all
with myself

What did I hide from her
what have I denied her
what losses suffered

how in this ignorant body
did she hide

waiting for her release
till uncontrollable light began to pour

•

from every wound and suture
and all the sacred openings

3.

Wartime.  We sit on warm
weathered, softening grey boards

the ladder glimmers where you told me
the leeches swim

I smell the flame
of kerosene    the pine

boards where we sleep side by side
in narrow cots

the night-meadow exhaling
its darkness    calling

child into woman
child into woman
woman

4.

Most of our love from the age of nine
took the form of jokes and mute

loyalty:    you fought a girl
who said she'd knock me down

we did each other's homework
wrote letters    kept in touch, untouching

lied about our lives: I wearing
the face of the proper marriage
                •

you the face of the independent woman
We cleaved to each other across that space

fingering webs
of love and estrangement till the day

the gynecologist touched your breast
and found a palpable hardness


5.

You played heroic, necessary
games with death

since in your neo-protestant tribe the void
was supposed not to exist

except as a fashionable concept
you had no traffic with

I wish you were here tonight   I want
to yell at you

*Don't accept*
*Don't give in*

But would I be meaning your brave
irreproachable life, you dean of women, or

your unfair, unfashionable, unforgivable
woman's death?


6.

You are every woman I ever loved
and disavowed
    •

a bloody incandescent chord strung out
across years, tracts of space

How can I reconcile this passion
with our modesty

your calvinist heritage
my girlhood frozen into forms

how can I go on this mission
without you

you, who might have told me
*everything you feel is true?*


7.


Time after time in dreams you rise
reproachful

once from a wheelchair pushed by your father
across a lethal expressway

Of all my dead it's you
who come to me unfinished

You left me amber beads
strung with turquoise from an Egyptian grave

I wear them wondering
How am I true to you?

I'm half-afraid to write poetry
for you    who never read it much

and I'm left laboring
with the secrets and the silence
            •

in plain language:    I never told you how I loved you
we never talked at your deathbed of your death

8.

One autumn evening in a train
catching the diamond-flash of sunset

in puddles along the Hudson
I thought:    *I understand*

*life and death now, the choices*
I didn't know your choice

or how by then you had no choice
how the body tells the truth in its rush of cells

Most of our love took the form
of mute loyalty

*we never spoke at your deathbed of your death*

but from here on
I want more crazy mourning, more howl, more keening

We stayed mute and disloyal
because we were afraid

I would have touched my fingers
to where your breasts had been
but we never did such things

1974–1977

# Natural Resources

1.

The core of the strong hill: not understood:
the mulch-heat of the underwood

where unforeseen the forest fire unfurls;
the heat, the privacy of the mines;

the rainbow laboring to extend herself
where neither men nor cattle understand,

arching her lusters over rut and stubble
purely to reach where she must go;

the emerald lying against the silver vein
waiting for light to reach it, breathing in pain;

the miner laboring beneath
the ray of the headlamp: a weight like death.

2.

The miner is no metaphor. She goes
into the cage like the rest, is flung

downward by gravity like them, must change
her body like the rest to fit a crevice

to work a lode
on her the pick hangs heavy, the bad air

lies thick, the mountain presses in on her
with boulder, timber, fog

slowly the mountain's dust descends
into the fibers of her lungs.

3.

The cage drops into the dark,
the routine of life goes on:

a woman turns a doorknob, but so slowly
so quietly, that no one wakes

and it is she alone who gazes
into the dark of bedrooms, ascertains

how they sleep, who needs her touch
what window blows the ice of February

into the room and who must be protected:
It is only she who sees; who was trained to see.

4.

*Could you imagine a world of women only,*
the interviewer asked. *Can you imagine*

*a world where women are absent.* (He believed
he was joking.) Yet I have to imagine

at one and the same moment, both. Because
I live in both. *Can you imagine,*

the interviewer asked, *a world of men?*
(He thought he was joking.) *If so, then,*

•

*a world where men are absent?*
Absently, wearily, I answered: Yes.


5.


The phantom of the man-who-would-understand,
the lost brother, the twin—

for him did we leave our mothers,
deny our sisters, over and over?

did we invent him, conjure him
over the charring log,

nights, late, in the snowbound cabin
did we dream or scry his face

in the liquid embers,
the man-who-would-dare-to-know-us?


6.


It was never the rapist:
it was the brother, lost,

the comrade/twin whose palm
would bear a lifeline like our own:

decisive, arrowy,
forked-lightning of insatiate desire

It was never the crude pestle, the blind
ramrod we were after:

merely a fellow-creature
with natural resources equal to our own
                •

7.

Meanwhile, another kind of being
was constructing itself, blindly

—a mutant, some have said:
the blood-compelled exemplar

of a "botched civilization"
as one of them called it

children picking up guns
for that is what it means to be a man

*We have lived with violence for seven years*
*It was not worth one single life—*

but the patriot's fist is at her throat,
her voice is in mortal danger

and that kind of being has lain in our beds
declaring itself our desire

requiring women's blood for life
a woman's breast to lay its nightmare on

8.

And that kind of being has other forms:
a passivity we mistake

—in the desperation of our search—
for gentleness

But gentleness is active
gentleness swabs the crusted stump

•

invents more merciful instruments
to touch the wound beyond the wound.

does not faint with disgust
will not be driven off

keeps bearing witness calmly
against the predator, the parasite

9.

I am tired of faintheartedness,
their having to be *exceptional*

to do what an ordinary woman
does in the course of things

I am tired of women stooping to half our height
to bring the essential vein to light

tired of the waste of what we bear
with such cost, such elation, into sight

(—for what becomes of what the miner probes
and carves from the mountain's body in her pain?)

10.

*This is what I am:* watching the spider
rebuild—"patiently", they say,

but I recognize in her
impatience—my own—

the passion to make and make again
where such unmaking reigns

the refusal to be a victim
*we have lived with violence so long*

&bull;

Am I to go on saying
for myself, for her

*This is my body,*
*take and destroy it?*

11.

The enormity of the simplest things:
in this cold barn tables are spread

with china saucers, shoehorns
of german silver, a gilt-edged book

that opens into a picture-frame—
a biscuit-tin of the thirties.

Outside, the north lies vast
with unshed snow, everything is

at once remote and familiar
each house contains what it must

women simmer carcasses
of clean-picked turkeys, store away

the cleaned cutglass and soak the linen cloths
Dark rushes early at the panes

12.

These things by women saved
are all we have of them

or of those dear to them
these ribboned letters, snapshots

faithfully glued for years
onto the scrapbook page
  •

these scraps, turned into patchwork,
doll-gowns, clean white rags

for stanching blood
the bride's tea-yellow handkerchief

the child's height penciled on the cellar door
In this cold barn we dream

a universe of humble things—
and without these, no memory

no faithfulness, no purpose for the future
no honor to the past

13.

There are words I cannot choose again:
*humanism    androgyny*

Such words have no shame in them, no diffidence
before the raging stoic grandmothers:

their glint is too shallow, like a dye
that does not permeate

the fibers of actual life
as we live it, now:

this fraying blanket with its ancient stains
we pull across the sick child's shoulder

or wrap around the senseless legs
of the hero trained to kill

this weaving, ragged because incomplete
we turn our hands to, interrupted
        •

over and over, handed down
unfinished, found in the drawer

of an old dresser in the barn,
her vanished pride and care

still urging us, urging on
our works, to close the gap

in the Great Nebula,
to help the earth deliver.

14.

The women who first knew themselves
miners, are dead. The rainbow flies

like a flying buttress from the walls
of cloud, the silver-and-green vein

awaits the battering of the pick
the dark lode weeps for light

My heart is moved by all I cannot save:
so much has been destroyed

I have to cast my lot with those
who age after age, perversely,

with no extraordinary power,
reconstitute the world.

1977

From

# *A Wild Patience Has Taken Me This Far*

1981

# Integrity

*the quality or state of being complete; unbroken*
*condition; entirety*
—Webster

A wild patience has taken me this far

as if I had to bring to shore
a boat with a spasmodic outboard motor
old sweaters, nets, spray-mottled books
tossed in the prow
some kind of sun burning my shoulder-blades.
Splashing the oarlocks. Burning through.
Your fore-arms can get scalded, licked with pain
in a sun blotted like unspoken anger
behind a casual mist.

The length of daylight
this far north, in this
forty-ninth year of my life
is critical.

The light is critical: of me, of this
long-dreamed, involuntary landing
on the arm of an inland sea.
The glitter of the shoal
depleting into shadow
I recognize: the stand of pines
violet-black really, green in the old postcard
but really I have nothing but myself
to go by; nothing
stands in the realm of pure necessity
except what my hands can hold.
    •

*Nothing but myself? . . . My selves.*
After so long, this answer.
As if I had always known
I steer the boat in, simply.
The motor dying on the pebbles
cicadas taking up the hum
dropped in the silence.

Anger and tenderness: my selves.
And now I can believe they breathe in me
as angels, not polarities.
Anger and tenderness: the spider's genius
to spin and weave in the same action
from her own body, anywhere—
even from a broken web.

The cabin in the stand of pines
is still for sale. I know this. Know the print
of the last foot, the hand that slammed and locked that door,
then stopped to wreathe the rain-smashed clematis
back on the trellis
for no one's sake except its own.
I know the chart nailed to the wallboards
the icy kettle squatting on the burner.
The hands that hammered in those nails
emptied that kettle one last time
are these two hands
and they have caught the baby leaping
from between trembling legs
and they have worked the vacuum aspirator
and stroked the sweated temples
and steered the boat here through this hot
mistblotted sunlight, critical light
imperceptibly scalding
the skin these hands will also salve.

1978

# For Memory

Old words:  *trust   fidelity*
Nothing new yet to take their place.

I rake leaves, clear the lawn, October grass
painfully green beneath the gold
and in this silent labor thoughts of you
start up
I hear your voice:   *disloyalty   betrayal*
stinging the wires

I stuff the old leaves into sacks
and still they fall and still
I see my work undone

One shivering rainswept afternoon
and the whole job to be done over

I can't know what you know
unless you tell me
there are gashes in our understandings
of this world
We came together in a common
fury of direction
barely mentioning difference
(what drew our finest hairs
to fire
the deep, difficult troughs
unvoiced)
I fell through a basement railing
the first day of school and cut my forehead open—
did I ever tell you? More than forty years
and I still remember smelling my own blood
like the smell of a new schoolbook
      •

And did you ever tell me
how your mother called you in from play
and from whom? To what? These atoms filmed by ordinary dust
that common life we each and all bent out of orbit from
to which we must return simply to say
*this is where I came from*
*this is what I knew*

The past is not a husk    yet change goes on

Freedom. It isn't once, to walk out
under the Milky Way, feeling the rivers
of light, the fields of dark—
freedom is daily, prose-bound, routine
remembering. Putting together, inch by inch
the starry worlds. From all the lost collections.

1979


# For Ethel Rosenberg

*Convicted, with her husband,*
*of "conspiracy to commit*
*espionage"; killed in the*
*electric chair June 19, 1953*

1.

Europe 1953:
throughout my random sleepwalk
the words

scratched on walls, on pavements
painted over railway arches
*Liberez les Rosenberg!*

•

Escaping from home I found
home everywhere:
the Jewish question, Communism

marriage itself
a question of loyalty
or punishment

my Jewish father writing me
letters of seventeen pages
finely inscribed harangues

questions of loyalty
and punishment
One week before my wedding

that couple gets the chair
the volts grapple her, don't
kill her fast enough

*Liberez les Rosenberg!*
I hadn't realized
our family arguments were so important

my narrow understanding
of crime    of punishment
no language for this torment

mystery of that marriage
always both faces
on every front page in the world

Something so shocking    so
unfathomable
it must be pushed aside

                •

2.

She sank however into my soul    A weight of sadness
I hardly can register how deep
her memory has sunk    that wife and mother

like so many
who seemed to get nothing out of any of it
except her children

that daughter    of a family
like so many
needing its female monster

she, actually wishing to be    *an artist*
wanting out of poverty
possibly also really wanting
                                        revolution

that woman    strapped in the chair
*no fear and no regrets*
charged by posterity

not with selling secrets to the Communists
but with wanting    *to distinguish
herself*    being a bad daughter    a bad mother

And I    walking to my wedding
by the same token a bad daughter    a bad sister
my forces focussed

on that hardly revolutionary effort
Her life and death    the possible
ranges of disloyalty

so painful    so unfathomable
they must be pushed aside
ignored for years
                    •

3.

Her mother testifies against her
Her brother testifies against her
After her death

she becomes a natural prey for pornographers
her death itself a scene
her body *sizzling    half-strapped    whipped like a sail*

She becomes the extremest victim
described nonetheless as *rigid of will*
what are her politics by then    no one knows

Her figure sinks into my soul
a drowned statue
sealed in lead

For years it has lain there    unabsorbed
first as part of that dead couple
on the front pages of the world    the week

I gave myself in marriage
then slowly severing    drifting apart
a separate death    a life unto itself

no longer *the Rosenbergs*
no longer the chosen scapegoat
the family monster

till I hear how she sang
a prostitute to sleep
in the Women's House of Detention

Ethel Greenglass Rosenberg    would you
have marched to take back the night
collected signatures
            •

for battered women who kill
What would you have to tell us
would you have burst the net

4.

Why do I even want to call her up
to console my pain    (she feels no pain at all)
why do I wish to put such questions

to ease myself    (she feels no pain at all
she    finally burned to death    like so many)
why all this exercise of hindsight?

since    if I imagine her at all
I have to imagine first
the pain inflicted on her    by women

*her mother testifies against her*
*her sister-in-law testifies against her*
and how she sees it

not the impersonal forces
not the historical reasons
why they might have hated her strength

If I have held her at arm's length till now
if I have still believed it was
my loyalty, my punishment at stake

if I dare imagine her surviving
I must be fair to what she must have lived through
I must allow her to be at last

political in her ways    not in mine
her urgencies perhaps    impervious to mine
defining revolution as she defines it
        •

or, bored to the marrow of her bones
with "politics"
bored with the vast boredom of long pain

small; tiny in fact; in her late sixties
liking her room    her private life
living alone perhaps

no one you could interview
maybe filling a notebook herself
with secrets she has never sold

1980


# Grandmothers

1. Mary Gravely Jones

We had no petnames, no diminutives for you,
always the formal guest under my father's roof:
you were "Grandmother Jones" and you visited rarely.
I see you walking up and down the garden,
restless, southern-accented, reserved, you did not seem
my mother's mother or anyone's grandmother.
You were Mary, widow of William, and no matriarch,
yet smoldering to the end with frustrate life,
ideas nobody listened to, least of all my father.
One summer night you sat with my sister and me
in the wooden glider long after twilight,
holding us there with streams of pent-up words.
You could quote every poet I had ever heard of,
had read *The Opium Eater,* Amiel and Bernard Shaw,
your green eyes looked clenched against opposition.
You married straight out of the convent school,
    •

your background was country, you left an unperformed
typescript of a play about Burr and Hamilton,
you were impotent and brilliant, no one cared
about your mind, you might have ended
elsewhere than in that glider
reciting your unwritten novels to the children.


2. Hattie Rice Rich

Your sweetness of soul was a mystery to me,
you who slip-covered chairs, glued broken china,
lived out of a wardrobe trunk in our guestroom
summer and fall, then took the Pullman train
in your darkblue dress and straw hat, to Alabama,
shuttling half-yearly between your son and daughter.
Your sweetness of soul was a convenience for everyone,
how you rose with the birds and children, boiled your own egg,
fished for hours on a pier, your umbrella spread,
took the street-car downtown shopping
endlessly for your son's whims, the whims of genius,
kept your accounts in ledgers, wrote letters daily.
All through World War Two the forbidden word
*Jewish* was barely uttered in your son's house;
your anger flared over inscrutable things.
Once I saw you crouched on the guestroom bed,
knuckles blue-white around the bedpost, sobbing
your one brief memorable scene of rebellion:
you didn't want to go back South that year.
You were never "Grandmother Rich" but "Anana";
you had money of your own but you were homeless,
Hattie, widow of Samuel, and no matriarch,
dispersed among the children and grandchildren.


3. Granddaughter

Easier to encapsulate your lives
in a slide-show of impressions given and taken,
         •

to play the child or victim, the projectionist,
easier to invent a script for each of you,
myself still at the center,
than to write words in which you might have found
yourselves, looked up at me and said
"Yes, I was like that; but I was something more. . . ."
Danville, Virginia; Vicksburg, Mississippi;
the "war between the states" a living memory
its aftermath the plague-town closing
its gates, trying to cure itself with poisons.
*I can almost touch that little town. . . .*
*a little white town rimmed with Negroes,*
*making a deep shadow on the whiteness.*
Born a white woman, Jewish or of curious mind
—twice an outsider, still believing in inclusion—
in those defended hamlets of half-truth
*broken in two by one strange idea,*
"blood" the all-powerful, awful theme—
what were the lessons to be learned? If I believe
the daughter of one of you—Amnesia was the answer.

1980

# The Spirit of Place

*—for Michelle Cliff*

I.

Over the hills in Shutesbury, Leverett
driving with you in spring     road
like a streambed unwinding downhill
fiddlehead ferns uncurling
spring peepers ringing sweet and cold
•

while we talk yet again
of dark and light, of blackness, whiteness, numbness
rammed through the heart like a stake
trying to pull apart the threads
from the dried blood of the old murderous uncaring

halting on bridges in bloodlight
where the freshets call out freedom
to frog-thrilling swamp, skunk-cabbage
trying to sense the conscience of these hills

knowing how the single-minded, pure
solutions bleached and dessicated
within their perfect flasks

for it was not enough to be New England
as every event since has testified:
New England's a shadow-country, always was

it was not enough to be for abolition
while the spirit of the masters
flickered in the abolitionist's heart

it was not enough to name ourselves anew
while the spirit of the masters
calls the freedwoman to forget the slave

*With whom do you believe your lot is cast?*
If there's a conscience in these hills
it hurls that question

unquenched, relentless, to our ears
wild and witchlike
ringing every swamp
     &bull;

II.

The mountain laurel in bloom
constructed like needlework
tiny half-pulled stitches piercing
flushed and stippled petals

here in these woods it grows wild
midsummer moonrise turns it opal
the night breathes with its clusters
protected species

meaning endangered
Here in these hills
this valley    we have felt
a kind of freedom

planting the soil    have known
hours of a calm, intense and mutual solitude
reading and writing
trying to clarify    connect

past and present    near and far
the Alabama quilt
the Botswana basket
history    the dark crumble

of last year's compost
filtering softly through your living hand
but here as well we face
instantaneous violence    ambush    male

dominion on a back road
to escape in a locked car    windows shut
skimming the ditch    your split-second
survival reflex taking on the world
                •

as it is    not as we wish it
as it is    not as we work for it
to be


III.


Strangers are an endangered species

In Emily Dickinson's house in Amherst
cocktails are served    the scholars
gather in celebration
their pious or clinical legends
festoon the walls like imitations
of period patterns

    (. . . *and, as I feared, my "life" was made a "victim"*)

The remnants pawed    the relics
the cult assembled in the bedroom

and you    whose teeth were set on edge by churches
resist your shrine
                escape
                      are found
nowhere
        unless in words
                (your own)

    *All we are strangers—dear—The world is not*
    *acquainted with us, because we are not acquainted*
    *with her. And Pilgrims!—Do you hesitate? and*
    *Soldiers oft—some of us victors, but those I do*
    *not see tonight owing to the smoke.—We are hungry,*
    *and thirsty, sometimes—We are barefoot—and cold—*

This place is large enough for both of us
the river-fog will do for privacy
this is my third and last address to you
      •

with the hands of a daughter I would cover you
from all intrusion    even my own
saying    rest to your ghost

with the hands of a sister I would leave your hands
open or closed as they prefer to lie
and ask no more of who or why or wherefore

with the hands of a mother I would close the door
on the rooms you've left behind
and silently pick up my fallen work

IV.

The river-fog will do for privacy
on the low road a breath
here, there, a cloudiness floating on the blacktop

sunflower heads turned black and bowed
the seas of corn a stubble
the old routes flowing north, if not to freedom

no human figure now in sight
(with whom do you believe your lot is cast?)
only the functional figure of the scarecrow

the cut corn, ground to shreds, heaped in a shape
like an Indian burial mound
a haunted-looking, ordinary thing

The work of winter starts fermenting in my head
how with the hands of a lover or a midwife
to hold back till the time is right

force nothing, be unforced
accept no giant miracles of growth
by counterfeit light
                •

trust roots, allow the days to shrink
give credence to these slender means
wait without sadness and with grave impatience

here in the north where winter has a meaning
where the heaped colors suddenly go ashen
where nothing is promised

learn what an underground journey
has been, might have to be; speak in a winter code
let fog, sleet, translate; wind, carry them.

V.

Orion plunges like a drunken hunter
over the Mohawk Trail    a parallelogram
slashed with two cuts of steel

A night so clear that every constellation
stands out from an undifferentiated cloud
of stars, a kind of aura

All the figures up there look violent to me
as a pogrom on Christmas Eve in some old country
I want our own earth    not the satellites, our

world as it is    if not as it might be
then as it is:    male dominion, gangrape, lynching, pogrom
the Mohawk wraiths in their tracts of leafless birch

watching:    will we do better?
The tests I need to pass are prescribed by the spirits
of place    who understand travel but not amnesia

The world as it is:    not as her users boast
damaged beyond reclamation by their using
Ourselves as we are    in these painful motions

•

of staying cognizant:    some part of us always
out beyond ourselves
knowing    knowing    knowing

Are we all in training for something we don't name?
to exact reparation for things
done long ago to us and to those who did not

survive what was done to them    whom we ought to honor
with grief    with fury    with action
On a pure night    on a night when pollution

seems absurdity when the undamaged planet seems to turn
like a bowl of crystal in black ether
they are the piece of us that lies out there
knowing    knowing    knowing

1980


# Frame

Winter twilight. She comes out of the lab-
oratory, last class of the day
a pile of notebooks slung in her knapsack, coat
zipped high against the already swirling
evening sleet. The wind is wicked and the
busses slower than usual. On her mind
is organic chemistry and the issue
of next month's rent and will it be possible to
bypass the professor with the coldest eyes
to get a reference for graduate school,
and whether any of them, even those who smile
can see, looking at her, a biochemist
or a marine biologist, which of the faces
    &bull;

can she trust to see her at all, either today
or in any future. The busses are worm-slow in the
quickly gathering dark. *I don't know her. I am
standing though somewhere just outside the frame
of all this, trying to see.* At her back
the newly finished building suddenly looks
like shelter, it has glass doors, lighted halls
presumably heat. The wind is wicked. She throws a
glance down the street, sees no bus coming and runs
up the newly constructed steps into the newly
constructed hallway. *I am standing all this time
just beyond the frame, trying to see.* She runs
her hand through the crystals of sleet about to melt
on her hair. She shifts the weight of the books
on her back. It isn't warm here exactly but it's
out of that wind. Through the glass
door panels she can watch for the bus through the thickening
weather. Watching so, she is not
watching for the white man who watches the building
who has been watching her. This is Boston 1979.
*I am standing somewhere at the edge of the frame
watching the man, we are both white, who watches the building
telling her to move on, get out of the hallway.
I can hear nothing because I am not supposed to be
present but I can see her gesturing
out toward the street at the wind-raked curb
I see her drawing her small body up
against the implied charges.* The man
goes away. Her body is different now.
It is holding together with more than a hint of fury
and more than a hint of fear. She is smaller, thinner
more fragile-looking than I am. *But I am not supposed to be
there. I am just outside the frame
of this action when the anonymous white man
returns with a white police officer.* Then she starts
to leave into the windraked night but already
the policeman is going to work, the handcuffs are on her
wrists he is throwing her down his knee has gone into

·

her breast he is dragging her down the stairs *I am unable*
*to hear a sound of all this all that I know is what*
*I can see from this position there is no soundtrack*
*to go with this and I understand at once*
*it is meant to be in silence that this happens*
in silence that he pushes her into the car
banging her head in silence that she cries out
in silence that she tries to explain she was only
waiting for a bus
in silence that he twists the flesh of her thigh
with his nails in silence that her tears begin to flow
that she pleads with the other policeman as if
he could be trusted to see her at all
in silence that in the precinct she refuses to give her name
in silence that they throw her into the cell
in silence that she stares him
straight in the face in silence that he sprays her
in her eyes with Mace in silence that she sinks her teeth
into his hand in silence that she is charged
with trespass assault and battery in
silence that at the sleet-swept corner her bus
passes without stopping and goes on
in silence. *What I am telling you*
*is told by a white woman who they will say*
*was never there. I say I am there.*

1980

From

*Your Native Land,*
*Your Life*

1986

# For the Record

The clouds and the stars didn't wage this war
the brooks gave no information
if the mountain spewed stones of fire into the river
it was not taking sides
the raindrop faintly swaying under the leaf
had no political opinions

and if here or there a house
filled with backed-up raw sewage
or poisoned those who lived there
with slow fumes, over years
the houses were not at war
nor did the tinned-up buildings

intend to refuse shelter
to homeless old women and roaming children
they had no policy to keep them roaming
or dying, no, the cities were not the problem
the bridges were non-partisan
the freeways burned, but not with hatred

Even the miles of barbed-wire
stretched around crouching temporary huts
designed to keep the unwanted
at a safe distance, out of sight
even the boards that had to absorb
year upon year, so many human sounds

so many depths of vomit, tears
slow-soaking blood
had not offered themselves for this
The trees didn't volunteer to be cut into boards
                    •

nor the thorns for tearing flesh
Look around at all of it

and ask whose signature
is stamped on the orders, traced
in the corner of the building plans
Ask where the illiterate, big-bellied
women were, the drunks and crazies,
the ones you fear most of all:     ask where you were

1983


# Virginia 1906

A white woman dreaming of innocence,
of a country childhood, apple-blossom driftings,
is held in a DC-10 above the purity
of a thick cloud ceiling in a vault of purest blue.
She feels safe.     Here, no one can reach her.
Neither men nor women have her in their power.

Because I have sometimes been her, because I am of her,
I watch her with eyes that blink away like a flash
cruelly, when she does what I don't want to see.
I am tired of innocence and its uselessness,
sometimes the dream of innocence beguiles me.
Nothing has told me how to think of her power.

Blurredly, apple-blossom drifts
across rough earth, small trees contort and twist
making their own shapes, wild.     Why should we love purity?
Can the woman in the DC-10 see this
and would she call this innocence?     If no one can reach her
she is drawing on unnamed, unaccountable power.
                •

This woman I have been and recognize
must know that beneath the quilt of whiteness lies
a hated nation, hers,
earth whose wet places call to mind
still-open wounds:        her country.
Do we love purity?    Where do we turn for power?

Knowing us as I do I cringe when she says
*But I was not culpable,*
*I was the victim, the girl, the youngest,*
*the susceptible one, I was sick,*
*the one who simply had to get out, and did*
: I am still trying how to think of her power.

And if she was forced, this woman, by the same
white Dixie boy who took for granted as prey
her ignored dark sisters?        What if at five years old
she was old to his fingers splaying her vulva open
what if forever after, in every record
she wants her name inscribed as *innocent*

and will not speak, refuses to know, can say
*I have been numb for years*
does not want to hear of any violation
like or unlike her own, as if the victim
can be innocent only in isolation
as if the victim dare not be intelligent

*(I have been numb for years):*   and if this woman
longs for an intact world, an intact soul,
longs for what we all long for, yet denies us all?
What has she smelled of power without once
tasting it in the mouth? For what protections
has she traded her wildness and the lives of others?

There is a porch in Salem, Virginia
that I have never seen, that may no longer stand,
                •

honeysuckle vines twisting above the talk,
a driveway full of wheeltracks, paths going down
to the orchards, apple and peach,
divisions so deep a wild child lost her way.

A child climbing an apple-tree in Virginia
refuses to come down, at last comes down
for a neighbor's lying bribe.    Now, if that child, grown old
feels safe in a DC-10 to above thick white clouds
and no one can reach her
and if that woman's child, another woman

chooses another way, yet finds the old vines
twisting across her path, the old wheeltracks
how does she stop dreaming the dream
of protection, how does she follow her own wildness
shedding the innocence, the childish power?
How does she keep from dreaming the old dreams?

1983

# For an Occupant

Did the fox speak to you?
Did the small brush-fires on the hillside
smoke her out?
Were you standing on the porch
not the kitchen porch      the front
one of poured concrete      full in the rising moon
and did she appear      wholly on her own
asking no quarter      wandering by
on impulse      up the drive      and on
into the pine-woods
but were you standing there
    •

at the moment of moon and burnished light
leading your own life      till she caught your eye
asking no charity
but did she speak to you?

1983


# North American Time

I

When my dreams showed signs
of becoming
politically correct
no unruly images
escaping beyond borders
when walking in the street I found my
themes cut out for me
knew what I would not report
for fear of enemies' usage
then I began to wonder

II

Everything we write
will be used against us
or against those we love.
These are the terms,
take them or leave them.
Poetry never stood a chance
of standing outside history.
One line typed twenty years ago
can be blazed on a wall in spraypaint
to glorify art as detachment

•

or torture of those we
did not love but also
did not want to kill

We move    but our words stand
become responsible
for more than we intended

and this is verbal privilege

III

Try sitting at a typewriter
one calm summer evening
at a table by a window
in the country, try pretending
your time does not exist
that you are simply you
that the imagination simply strays
like a great moth, unintentional
try telling yourself
you are not accountable
to the life of your tribe
the breath of your planet

IV

It doesn't matter what you think.
Words are found responsible
all you can do is choose them
or choose
to remain silent.    Or, you never had a choice,
which is why the words that do stand
are responsible

and this is verbal privilege
                •

V

Suppose you want to write
of a woman braiding
another woman's hair—
straight down, or with beads and shells
in three-strand plaits or corn-rows—
you had better know the thickness
the length    the pattern
why she decides to braid her hair
how it is done to her
what country it happens in
what else happens in that country

You have to know these things


VI

Poet, sister:    words—
whether we like it or not—
stand in a time of their own.
No use protesting    *I wrote that*
*before Kollontai was exiled*
*Rosa Luxemburg, Malcolm,*
*Anna Mae Aquash, murdered,*
*before Treblinka, Birkenau,*
*Hiroshima, before Sharpeville,*
*Biafra, Bangla Desh, Boston,*
*Atlanta, Soweto, Beirut, Assam*
—those faces, names of places
sheared from the almanac
of North American time


VII

I am thinking this in a country
where words are stolen out of mouths
        •

as bread is stolen out of mouths
where poets don't go to jail
for being poets, but for being
dark-skinned, female, poor.
I am writing this in a time
when anything we write
can be used against those we love
where the context is never given
though we try to explain, over and over
For the sake of poetry at least
I need to know these things

VIII

Sometimes, gliding at night
in a plane over New York City
I have felt like some messenger
called to enter, called to engage
this field of light and darkness.
A grandiose idea, born of flying.
But underneath the grandiose idea
is the thought that what I must engage
after the plane has raged onto the tarmac
after climbing my old stairs, sitting down
at my old window
is meant to break my heart and reduce me to silence.

IX

In North America time stumbles on
without moving, only releasing
a certain North American pain.
Julia de Burgos wrote:
*That my grandfather was a slave*
*is my grief; had he been a master*
*that would have been my shame.*
A poet's words, hung over a door
                •

in North America, in the year
nineteen-eighty-three.
The almost-full moon rises
timelessly speaking of change
out of the Bronx, the Harlem River
the drowned towns of the Quabbin
the pilfered burial mounds
the toxic swamps, the testing-grounds

and I start to speak again.

1983

# Blue Rock

*For Myriam Díaz-Diocaretz*

Your chunk of lapis-lazuli shoots its stain
blue into the wineglass on the table

the full moon moving up the sky is plain
as the dead rose and the live buds on one stem

No, this isn't Persian poetry I'm quoting:
all this is here in North America

where I sit trying to kindle fire
from what's already on fire:

the light of a blue rock from Chile swimming
in the apricot liquid called "eye of the swan".

•

This is a chunk of your world, a piece of its heart:
split from the rest, does it suffer?

You needn't tell me.    Sometimes I hear it singing
by the waters of Babylon, in a strange land

sometimes it just lies heavy in my hand
with the heaviness of silent seismic knowledge

a blue rock in a foreign land, an exile
excised but never separated

from the gashed heart, its mountains,
winter rains, language, native sorrow.


At the end of the twentieth century
cardiac graphs of torture reply to poetry

line by line:        in North America
the strokes of the stylus continue

the figures of terror are reinvented
all night, after I turn the lamp off, blotting

wineglass, rock and roses, leaving pages
like this scrawled with mistakes and love,

falling asleep; but the stylus does not sleep,
cruelly the drum revolves, cruelty writes its name.


Once when I wrote poems they did not change
left overnight on the page
•

they stayed as they were and daylight broke
on the lines, as on the clotheslines in the yard

heavy with clothes forgotten or left out
for a better sun next day

But now I know what happens while I sleep
and when I wake the poem has changed:

the facts have dilated it, or cancelled it;
and in every morning's light, your rock is there.

1985


# *from* Contradictions: Tracking Poems

1.

Look:    this is January    the worst onslaught
is ahead of us    Don't be lured
by these soft grey afternoons    these sunsets cut
from pink and violet tissue-paper    by the thought
the days are lengthening
Don't let the solstice fool you:
our lives will always be
a stew of contradictions
the worst moment of winter can come in April
when the peepers are stubbornly still    and our bodies
plod on without conviction
and our thoughts cramp down before the sheer
arsenal of everything that tries us:
this battering, blunt-edged life
        •

2.

Heart of cold.    Bones of cold.    Scalp of cold.
the grey        the black        the blond        the red
hairs on a skull of cold.        Within that skull
the thought of war        the sovereign thought
the coldest of all thought.    Dreaming shut down
everything kneeling down to cold        intelligence
smirking with cold        memory
squashed and frozen cold        breath
half held-in for cold.        The freezing people
of a freezing nation        eating
luxury food or garbage
frozen tongues licking the luxury meat
or the pizza-crust        the frozen eyes
welded to other eyes        also frozen
the cold hands trying to stroke        the coldest sex.
Heart of cold        Sex of cold        Intelligence of cold
My country        wedged fast in history
stuck in the ice


3.

My mouth hovers across your breasts
in the short grey winter afternoon
in this bed        we are delicate
and tough        so hot with joy we amaze ourselves
tough        and delicate        we play rings
around each other        our daytime candle burns
with its peculiar light        and if the snow
begins to fall outside        filling the branches
and if the night falls        without announcement
these are the pleasures of winter
sudden, wild and delicate        your fingers
exact        my tongue exact at the same moment
stopping to laugh at a joke
my love        hot on your scent        on the cusp of winter
        •

6.

Dear Adrienne:
                    I'm calling you up tonight
as I might call up a friend        as I might call up a ghost
to ask what you intend to do
with the rest of your life.    Sometimes you act
as if you have all the time there is.
I worry about you when I see this.
The prime of life, old age
aren't what they used to be;
making a good death isn't either,
now you can walk around the corner of a wall
and see a light
that already has blown your past away.
Somewhere in Boston        beautiful literature
is being read around the clock
by writers        to signify
their dislike of this.
I hope you've got something in mind.
I hope you have some idea
about the rest of your life.
                              In sisterhood,


                                        Adrienne


7.

Dear Adrienne,
                    I feel signified by pain
from my breastbone through my left shoulder down
through my elbow into my wrist is a thread of pain
I am typing this instead of writing by hand
because my wrist on the right side
blooms and rushes with pain
like a neon bulb
You ask me how I'm going to live
        •

the rest of my life
Well, nothing is predictable with pain
Did the old poets write of this?
—in its odd spaces, free,
many have sung and battled—
But I'm already living the rest of my life
not under conditions of my choosing
wired     into pain
                    rider on the slow train


                                        Yours, Adrienne


10.


Night       over the great and the little worlds
of Brooklyn       the shredded communities
in Chicago       Argentina       Poland
in Holyoke Massachusetts       Amsterdam       Manchester
     England
Night falls       the day of atonement begins
in how many divided hearts       how many defiant lives
Toronto       Managua       St. Johnsbury
and the great and little worlds of the women
Something ancient passes across the earth
lifting the dust of the blasted ghettos
You ask if I will eat and I say, Yes,
I have never fasted
but something crosses my life
not a shadow       the reflection of a fire


11.


I came out of the hospital like a woman
who'd watched a massacre
not knowing how to tell
my adhesions       the lingering infections
from the pain on the streets
          •

In my room on Yom Kippur they took me off morphine
I saw shadows on the wall      the dying and the dead
They said Christian Phalangists did it
then Kol Nidre on the radio          and my own
unhoused spirit      trying to find a home
Was it then or another day
in what order did it happen
I thought      *They call this elective surgery*
*but we all have died of this.*


12.


Violence as purification:      the one idea.
One massacre great enough to undo another
one last-ditch operation to solve the problem
of the old operation that was bungled
Look:    I have lain on their tables under their tools
under their drugs      from the center of my body
a voice bursts      against these methods
(wherever you made a mistake
batter with radiation      defoliate      cut away)
and yes, there are merciful debridements
but burns turn into rotting flesh
for reasons of vengeance and neglect.
I have been too close to septic too many times
to play with either violence or non-violence.


14.


Lately in my dreams I hear long sentences
meaningless in ordinary American
like, *Your mother, too, was a missionary of poets*
and in another dream one of my old teachers
shows me a letter of reference
he has written for me, in a language
I know to be English but cannot understand,
telling me it's in "transformational grammar"
    •

and that the student who typed the letter
does not understand this grammar either.
Lately I dreamed about my father,
how I found him, alive, seated on an old chair.
I think what he said to me was,
*You don't know how lonely I am.*


15.


You who think I find words for everything,
and you for whom I write this,
how can I show you what I'm barely
coming into possession of, invisible luggage
of more than fifty years, looking at first
glance like everyone else's, turning up
at the airport carousel
and the waiting for it, knowing what nobody
would steal must eventually come round—
feeling obsessed, peculiar, longing?


18.


The problem, unstated till now, is how
to live in a damaged body
in a world where pain is meant to be gagged
uncured     un-grieved-over     The problem is
to connect, without hysteria, the pain
of any one's body with the pain of the body's world
For it is the body's world
they are trying to destroy forever
The best world is the body's world
filled with creatures     filled with dread
misshapen so     yet the best we have
our raft among the abstract worlds
and how I longed to live on this earth
walking her boundaries     never counting the cost
                    •

20.

The tobacco fields lie fallow     the migrant pickers
no longer visible
where undocumented intelligences travailed
on earth they had no stake in
though the dark leaves growing beneath white veils
were beautiful     and the barns opened out like fans
All this of course could have been done differently
This valley itself:     one more contradiction
the paradise fields     the brute skyscrapers
the pesticidal wells

I have been wanting for years
to write a poem     equal to these
material forces
and I have always failed
I wasn't looking for a muse
only a reader by whom     I could not be mistaken

22.

In a bald skull sits our friend     in a helmet
of third-degree burns
her quizzical melancholy grace
her irreplaceable self     in utter peril
In the radioactive desert walks a woman
in a black dress     white-haired     steady
as the luminous hand of a clock
in circles she walks     knitting
and unknitting her scabbed fingers
Her face is expressionless     shall we pray to her
shall we speak of the loose pine-needles     how they shook
like the pith of country summers
from the sacks of pitchblende ore in the tin-roofed shack
where it all began
Shall we accuse her of denial
          •

first of the self       then of the mixed virtue
of the purest science       shall we be wise for her
in hindsight       shall we scream *It has come to this*
Shall we praise her       shall we let her wander
the atomic desert       in peace?


23.

You know the Government must have pushed them to settle,
the chemical industries       and pay
that hush-money to the men
who landed out there at twenty       not for belief
but because of who they were       and were called psychos
when they said their bodies contained dioxin
like memories they didn't want to keep
whose kids came out deformed
You know nothing has changed       no respect or grief
for the losers of a lost war everyone hated
nobody sent them to school like heroes
if they started sueing for everything that was done
there would be no end       there would be a beginning
My country       wedged fast in history
stuck in the ice


26.

You:    air-driven       reft       from the tuber-bitten soil
that was your portion       from the torched-out village
the Marxist study-group       the Zionist cell
café or *cheder*       Zaddik or Freudian       straight or gay
woman or man       O you
stripped       bared       appalled
stretched to mere spirit       yet still physical
your irreplaceable knowledge       lost
at the mud-slick bottom of the world
how you held fast       with your bone-meal fingers
to yourselves       each other       and strangers
       •

how you touched    held-up from falling
what was already half-cadaver
how your life-cry taunted extinction
with its wild, crude    *so what?*
Grief for you has rebellion at its heart
it cannot simply mourn
You:    air-driven:    reft:    are yet our teachers
trying to speak to us in sleep
trying to help us wake

27.

The Tolstoyans    the Afro-American slaves
knew this:    you could be killed
for teaching people to read and write
I used to think the worst affliction
was to be forbidden pencil and paper
well, Ding Ling recited poems to prison walls
for years of the Cultural Revolution
and truly, the magic of written characters
looms and dwindles    shrinks small    grows swollen
depending on where you stand
and what is in your hand
and who can read and why
I think now the worst affliction
is not to know who you are or have been
I have learned this in part
from writers    Reading and writing
aren't sacred    yet people have been killed
as if they were

29.

You who think I find words for everything
this is enough for now
cut it short    cut loose from my words
             •

You for whom I write this
in the night hours when the wrecked cartilage
sifts round the mystical jointure of the bones
when the insect of detritus crawls
from shoulder to elbow to wristbone
remember:    the body's pain and the pain on the streets
are not the same    but you can learn
from the edges that blur    O you who love clear edges
more than anything    watch the edges that blur

1983–1985

# From

# *Time's Power*

1989

# In a Classroom

Talking of poetry, hauling the books
arm-full to the table where the heads
bend or gaze upward, listening, reading aloud,
talking of consonants, elision,
caught in the how, oblivious of why:
I look in your face, Jude,
neither frowning nor nodding,
opaque in the slant of dust-motes over the table:
a presence like a stone, if a stone were thinking
*What I cannot say, is me. For that I came.*

1986


# The Novel

All winter you went to bed early, drugging yourself on *War and
Peace*
Prince Andrei's cold eyes taking in the sky from the battlefield
were your eyes, you went walking wrapped in his wound
like a padded coat against the winds from the two rivers
You went walking in the streets as if you were ordinary
as if you hadn't been pulling with your raw mittened hand
on the slight strand that held your tattered mind
blown like an old stocking from a wire
on the wind between two rivers.
                              All winter you asked nothing
of that book though it lay heavy on your knees
you asked only for a shed skin, many skins in which to walk
you were old woman, child, commander
        •

you watched Natasha grow into a neutered thing
you felt your heart go still while your eyes swept the pages
you felt the pages thickening to the left and on the right-
hand growing few, you knew the end was coming
you knew beyond the ending lay
your own, unwritten life

1986


# Children Playing Checkers
# at the Edge of the Forest

Two green-webbed chairs
                              a three-legged stool between
Your tripod
                    Spears of grass
                                        longer than your bare legs
cast shadows on your legs
                              drawn up
                                        from the red-and-black
cardboard squares
                    the board of play
                                        the board of rules
But you're not playing, you're talking
                                        It's midsummer
and greater rules are breaking
                              It's the last
innocent summer you will know
                              and I
will go on awhile pretending that's not true

When I have done pretending
                              I can see this:
        •

the depth of the background
                         shadows
                                   not of one moment only
erased and charcoaled in again
                         year after year

how the tree looms back behind you
the first tree of the forest
                         the last tree
from which the deer step out
                         from protection
                                        the first tree
into dreadfulness
                 The last and the first tree

1987


# The Desert as
# Garden of Paradise

1.

Guard the knowledge
from the knowledgeable,
those who gobble:
make it unpalatable.

Stars in this place
might look
distant to me as you,
to you as me.

Monotheism. Where it began.
But all the spirits, too.
Desert says: What you believe
        •

I can prove. I: amaranth flower,
I: metamorphic rock, I: burrow,
I: water-drop in tilted catchment,
I: vulture, I: driest thorn.

Rocks in a trance. Escaped
from the arms of other rocks.
Roads leading to gold and to false gold.

2.

I ask you to sing, Chavela, in the desert
on tapes pirated from smuggled LP's
I bring you here with me: I ask you to sing

It's not for me, your snarling contralto
caught on a backdrop of bitter guitar
not for me    yet I pray let me listen

I don't pray often    Never to male or female
sometimes to music or the flask of sunset
quick winter evenings    draining into the ground

our blood is mixed in, borderland magenta
and vermilion, never to become one
yet what we're singing, dying in, that color

two-worlded, never one    Where from bars
lit by candle and earthquake your music finds me
whom it didn't look for    This is why I ask you

when the singing escapes the listener and goes
from the throat to where the mountains hang in chains
as if they never listened    why the song

wants so much to go where no song has ever gone.
                    •

3.

In this pale clear light where all mistakes are bathed
this afterglow of westernness
I write to you, head wrapped in your darkred scarf

framed by the sharp spines of the cholla
you love, the cruel blonde
spirit of the Mohave blossoming

in the spring twilights
of much earlier ages
Off at this distance I'm safe

to conjure the danger
you undergo daily, chin outthrust
eyelid lowered against the storm

that takes in an inkling whole ranches down
with the women the men and the children
the horses and cattle

—that much, flash-flood, lightning
all that had been done right, gone to hell
all crimes washed down the gulch

of independence, lost horse trail
Well, this was your country, Malinche
and is, where you choose to speak

4.

Every drought-resistant plant has its own story
each had to learn to live
with less and less water, each would have loved
                 •

to laze in long soft rains, in the quiet drip
after the thunderstorm
each could do without deprivation

but where drought is the epic then there must be some
who persist, not by species-betrayal
but by changing themselves

minutely, by a constant study
of the price of continuity
a steady bargain with the way things are


5.


Then there were those, white-skinned
riding on camels
fast under scorching skies
their lives a tome of meaning
holding all this in fief:
star-dragged heavens, embroidered saddle-bags
coffee boiled up in slim urns
the salt, the oil, the roads
linking Europe with Asia
Crusaders, Legionnaires
desert-rats of empire
sucking the kid's bones, drunk with meaning
fucking the Arab, killing the Jew


6.


*Deutsches Blut,* Ahmad the Arab
tells Arnold the Jew
tapping the blue
veins of his own brown wrist
in his own walled garden
spread with figured carpets
summer, starlight, 1925
                    •

Was it the Crusader line?
Did they think it made them brothers?
Arnold the Jew my father
told me the story, showed me
his photograph of Ahmad: *Deutsches Blut*


7.


Then there were those, black-robed
on horseback, tracing the great plateaus
cut by arroyos, cleft by ravines
facing Sierra San Pedro San Mártir
a fixed bar welding Baja California
to the mainland north:
*a land the most unfortunate*
*ungrateful and miserable of this world*
Padre Miguel Venegas wrote
yet they ordered the missions raised
from fragile ramadas
the thin stream drawn from the watering-hole
into gardens of fig, palm, sugarcane
tried to will what cannot be willed
killed many in the trying:
unpacked smallpox, measles, typhus
from the chests with the linens and chalices
packed the sufferers in plague-ridden rooms
baptized in one village walk
all the children, who then died.
(San Ignacio!  Soledad!)
There were those: convinced the material
was base, the humanity less
—*Out of what can I bring forth a Christian soul?*
*For these, naked and dark*
*I come to do the work of Cross and Crown?*
winning hearts and minds
peeling the prickly pear
and dousing it in wine
        •

8.

What would it mean to think
you are part of a generation
that simply must pass on?
What would it mean to live
in the desert, try to live
a human life, something
to hand on to the children
to take up to the Land?
What would it mean to think
you were born in chains and only time,
nothing you can do
could redeem the slavery
you were born into?

9.

Out of a knot of deadwood
on ghostly grey-green stems
the nightblooming cereus opens
On a still night, under Ursa Major
the tallest saguaro cracks with cold
The eaters of herbs are eaten
the carnivores' bones fall down
and scavengers pick them clean
This is not for us, or if it is
with whom, and where, is the covenant?

10.

When it all stands clear you come to love
the place you are:
*the bundle of bare sticks soaked*
*with resin*
always, and never, a bush on fire
*the blue sky without tale or text*

•

*and without meaning*
*the great swing of the horizontal circle*
Miriam, Aaron, Moses
are somewhere else, marching
You learn to live without prophets
without legends
to live just where you are
your burning bush, your seven-branched candlestick
the ocotillo in bloom


11.


What's sacred is nameless
moves in the eyeflash
holds still in the circle
of the great arid basin
once watered and fertile
probes outward through twigbark
a green ghost inhabiting
dormant stick, abstract thorn
What's sacred is singular:
out of this dry fork, this
*wreck of perspective*
what's sacred tries itself
one more time


1987–1988

# Delta

If you have taken this rubble for my past
raking through it for fragments you could sell
know that I long ago moved on
deeper into the heart of the matter

If you think you can grasp me, think again:
my story flows in more than one direction
a delta springing from the riverbed
with its five fingers spread

1987

# Dreamwood

In the old, scratched, cheap wood of the typing stand
there is a landscape, veined, which only a child can see
or the child's older self,
a woman dreaming when she should be typing
the last report of the day.     If this were a map,
she thinks, a map laid down to memorize
because she might be walking it, it shows
ridge upon ridge fading into hazed desert,
here and there a sign of aquifers
and one possible watering-hole.     If this were a map
it would be the map of the last age of her life,
not a map of choices but a map of variations
on the one great choice. It would be the map by which
she could see the end of touristic choices,

•

of distances blued and purpled by romance,
by which she would recognize that poetry
isn't revolution but a way of knowing
why it must come.    If this cheap, massproduced
wooden stand from the Brooklyn Union Gas Co.,
massproduced yet durable, being here now,
is what it is yet a dream-map
so obdurate, so plain,
she thinks, the material and the dream can join
and that is the poem and that is the late report.

1987

# Harpers Ferry

Where do I get this landscape? Two river-roads
glittering at each other's throats, the Virginia mountains fading
across the gorge, the October-shortened sun, the wooden town,
rebellion sprouting encampments in the hills
and a white girl running away from home
who will have to see it all. But where do I get this, how
do I know how the light quails from the trembling
waters, autumn goes to ash from ridge to ridge
how behind the gunmetal pines the guns
are piled, the sun drops, and the watchfires burn?

I know the men's faces tremble like smoky
crevices in a cave where candle-stumps have been stuck
on ledges by fugitives. The men are dark and sometimes pale
like her, their eyes pouched or blank or squinting, all by now
are queer, outside, and out of bounds and have no membership
in any brotherhood but this: where power is handed from
the ones who can get it to the ones
who have been refused. It's a simple act,

•

to steal guns and hand them to the slaves. Who would have
                    thought it.

Running away from home is slower than her quick feet thought
and this is not the vague and lowering North, ghostland of deeper
                    snows
than she has ever pictured
but this is one exact and definite place,
a wooden village at the junction of two rivers
two trestle bridges hinged and splayed,
low houses crawling up the mountains.

Suppose she slashes her leg on a slashed pine's tooth, ties the leg
                    in a kerchief
knocks on the door of a house, the first on the edge of town
has to beg water, won't tell her family name, afraid someone will
                    know her family face
lies with her throbbing leg on the vined verandah where the woman
                    of the house
wanted her out of there, that was clear
yet with a stern and courteous patience leaned above her
with cold tea, water from the sweetest spring, mint from the same
                    source
later with rags wrung from a boiling kettle
and studying, staring eyes. Eyes ringed with watching. A peachtree
                    shedding yellowy leaves
and a houseful of men who keep off. So great a family of men, and
                    then this woman
who wanted her gone yet stayed by her, watched over her.
But this girl is expert in overhearing
and one word leaps off the windowpanes like the crack of dawn,
the translation of the babble of two rivers. What does this girl
with her little family quarrel, know about arsenals?
Everything she knows is wrapped up in her leg
without which she won't get past Virginia, though she's running
                    north.
        •

Whatever gave the girl the idea you could run away
from a family quarrel? Displace yourself, when nothing else
would change? It wasn't books:

it was half-overheard, a wisp of talk:
*escape   flight   free soil*
softing past her shoulder

She has never dreamed of arsenals, though
she's a good rifle-shot, taken at ten
by her brothers, hunting

and though they've climbed her over and over
leaving their wet clots in her sheets
on her new-started maidenhair

she has never reached for a gun to hold them off
for guns are the language of the strong to the weak
—How many squirrels have crashed between her sights

what vertebrae cracked at her finger's signal
what wings staggered through the boughs
whose eyes, ringed and treed, has she eyed as prey?

There is a strategy of mass flight
a strategy of arming
questions of how, of when, of where:

the arguments soak through the walls
of the houseful of men where running from home
the white girl lies in her trouble.


There are things overheard and things unworded, never sung
or pictured, things that happen silently
as the peachtree's galactic blossoms open in mist, the frost-star
hangs in the stubble, the decanter of moonlight pours its mournless
                    liquid down
    •

steadily on the solstice fields
the cotton swells in its boll and you feel yourself engorged,
                    unnameable
you yourself feel encased and picked-open, you feel yourself
                    unenvisaged
There is no quarrel possible in this silence
You stop yourself listening for a word that will not be spoken:
                    listening instead to the overheard
fragments, phrases melting on air: *No more   Many thousand go*
And you know they are leaving as fast as they can, you whose child's
                    eye followed each face wondering
not how could they leave but when: you knew they would leave
and so could you but not with them, you were not their child, they
                    had their own children
you could leave the house where you were daughter, sister, prey
picked open and left to silence, you could leave alone

This would be my scenario of course: that the white girl understands
what I understand and more, that the leg torn in flight
had not betrayed her, had brought her to another point of struggle
that when she takes her place she is clear in mind and her anger
true with the training of her hand and eye, her leg cured on the
                    porch of history
ready for more than solitary defiance. That when the General passes
                    through
in her blazing headrag, this girl knows her for Moses, pleads to
                    stand with the others in the shortened light
accepts the scrutiny, the steel-black gaze; but Moses passes and is
                    gone to her business elsewhere
leaving the men to theirs, the girl to her own.
But who would she take as leader?
would she fade into the woods
will she die in an *indefensible position*, a *miscarried raid*
does she lose the family face at last
pressed into a gully above two rivers, does Shenandoah or Potomac
                    carry her
        •

north or south, will she wake in the mining camps to stoke the
                                    stoves
and sleep at night with her rifle blue and loyal under her hand
does she ever forget how they left, how they taught her leaving?

1988

From

*An Atlas of the Difficult World*

1991

# *from* An Atlas of the Difficult World

I

A dark woman, head bent, listening for something
—a woman's voice, a man's voice or
voice of the freeway, night after night, metal streaming downcoast
past eucalyptus, cypress, agribusiness empires
THE SALAD BOWL OF THE WORLD, gurr of small planes
dusting the strawberries, each berry picked by a hand
in close communion, strawberry blood on the wrist,
Malathion in the throat, communion,
the hospital at the edge of the fields,
prematures slipping from unsafe wombs,
the labor and delivery nurse on her break watching
planes dusting rows of pickers.
Elsewhere declarations are made:    at the sink
rinsing strawberries flocked and gleaming, fresh from market
one says: "On the pond this evening is a light
finer than my mother's handkerchief
received from her mother, hemmed and initialled
by the nuns in Belgium."
One says:    "I can lie for hours
reading and listening to music. But sleep comes hard.
I'd rather lie awake and read."    One writes:
"Mosquitoes pour through the cracks
in this cabin's walls, the road
in winter is often impassable,
I live here so I don't have to go out and act,
I'm trying to hold onto my life, it feels like nothing."
One says: "I never knew from one day to the next
where it was coming from:    I had to make my life happen
from day to day.    Every day an emergency.
Now I have a house, a job from year to year.
                    •

What does that make me?"
In the writing workshop a young man's tears
wet the frugal beard he's grown to go with his poems
hoping they have redemption stored
in their lines, maybe will get him home free.     In the classroom
eight-year-old faces are grey.     The teacher knows which children
have not broken fast that day,
remembers the Black Panthers spooning cereal.

---

I don't want to hear how he beat her after the earthquake,
tore up her writing, threw the kerosene
lantern into her face waiting
like an unbearable mirror of his own.     I don't
want to hear how she finally ran from the trailer
how he tore the keys from her hands, jumped into the truck
and backed it into her.     I don't want to think
how her guesses betrayed her—that he meant well, that she
was really the stronger and ought not to leave him
to his own apparent devastation.     I don't want to know
wreckage, dreck and waste, but these are the materials
and so are the slow lift of the moon's belly
over wreckage, dreck, and waste, wild treefrogs calling in
another season, light and music still pouring over
our fissured, cracked terrain.

---

Within two miles of the Pacific rounding
this long bay, sheening the light for miles
inland, floating its fog through redwood rifts and over
strawberry and artichoke fields, its bottomless mind
returning always to the same rocks, the same cliffs, with
ever-changing words, always the same language
—this is where I live now.     If you had known me
once, you'd still know me now though in a different
light and life.     This is no place you ever knew me.

But it would not surprise you
to find me here, walking in fog, the sweep of the great ocean
          •

eluding me, even the curve of the bay, because as always
I fix on the land.     I am stuck to earth.     What I love here
is old ranches, leaning seaward, lowroofed spreads between rocks
small canyons running through pitched hillsides
liveoaks twisted on steepness, the eucalyptus avenue leading
to the wrecked homestead, the fogwreathed heavy-chested cattle
on their blond hills.     I drive inland over roads
closed in wet weather, past shacks hunched in the canyons
roads that crawl down into darkness and wind into light
where trucks have crashed and riders of horses tangled
to death with lowstruck boughs.     These are not the roads
you knew me by.     But the woman driving, walking, watching
for life and death, is the same.


II


Here is a map of our country:
here is the Sea of Indifference, glazed with salt
This is the haunted river flowing from brow to groin
we dare not taste its water
This is the desert where missiles are planted like corms
This is the breadbasket of foreclosed farms
This is the birthplace of the rockabilly boy
This is the cemetery of the poor
who died for democracy     This is a battlefield
from a nineteenth-century war     the shrine is famous
This is the sea-town of myth and story     when the fishing fleets
went bankrupt     here is where the jobs were     on the pier
processing frozen fishsticks     hourly wages and no shares
These are other battlefields     Centralia     Detroit
here are the forests primeval     the copper     the silver lodes
These are the suburbs of acquiescence     silence rising fumelike
          from the streets
This is the capital of money and dolor whose spires
flare up through air inversions whose bridges are crumbling
whose children are drifting blind alleys pent
between coiled rolls of razor wire
     •

I promised to show you a map you say but this is a mural
then yes let it be    these are small distinctions
where do we see it from is the question

IV

Late summers, early autumns, you can see something that binds
the map of this country together:    the girasol, orange gold-
                petalled
with her black eye, laces the roadsides from Vermont to
                California
runs the edges of orchards, chain-link fences
milo fields and malls, schoolyards and reservations
truckstops and quarries, grazing ranges, graveyards
of veterans, graveyards of cars hulked and sunk, her tubers the
                jerusalem artichoke
that has fed the Indians, fed the hobos, could feed us all.
Is there anything in the soil, cross-country, that makes for
a plant so generous?    *Spendthrift* we say, as if
accounting nature's waste.    Ours darkens
the states to their strict borders, flushes
down borderless streams, leaches from lakes to the curdled foam
down by the riverside.

Waste.    Waste.    The watcher's eye put out, hands of the
                builder severed, brain of the maker starved
those who could bind, join, reweave, cohere, replenish
now at risk in this segregate republic
locked away out of sight and hearing, out of mind, shunted aside
those needed to teach, advise, persuade, weigh arguments
those urgently needed for the work of perception
work of the poet, the astronomer, the historian, the architect of
                new streets
work of the speaker who also listens
meticulous delicate work of reaching the heart of the desperate
                woman, the desperate man
—never-to-be-finished, still unbegun work of repair—it cannot
        •

be done without them
and where are they now?

V

Catch if you can your country's moment, begin
where any calendar's ripped-off: Appomattox
Wounded Knee, Los Alamos, Selma, the last airlift from Saigon
the ex-Army nurse hitch-hiking from the debriefing center; medal
        of spit on the veteran's shoulder
—catch if you can this unbound land these states without a cause
earth of despoiled graves and grazing these embittered brooks
these pilgrim ants pouring out from the bronze eyes, ears,
        nostrils,
the mouth of Liberty
                *over the chained bay waters*
                                San Quentin:
once we lost our way and drove in under the searchlights to the
        gates
end of visiting hours, women piling into cars
the bleak glare aching over all
                Where are we moored?    What
                are the bindings?    What be-
                hooves us?

Driving the San Francisco—Oakland Bay Bridge
no monument's in sight but fog
prowling Angel Island muffling Alcatraz
poems in Cantonese inscribed on fog
no icon lifts a lamp here
history's breath blotting the air
over Gold Mountain    a transfer
of patterns like the transfer of African appliqué
to rural Alabama    voices alive in legends, curses
tongue-lashings
                poems on a weary wall
And when light swivels off Angel Island and Alcatraz
    •

when the bays leap into life
                              views of the Palace of Fine Arts,
                         TransAmerica
when sunset bathes the three bridges
                                   still
old ghosts crouch hoarsely whispering
under Gold Mountain

———————

North and east of the romantic headlands there are roads into tule
                   fog
places where life is cheap poor quick unmonumented
Rukeyser would have guessed it coming West for the opening
of the great red bridge    *There are roads to take* she wrote
*when you think of your country*    driving south
to West Virginia Gauley Bridge silicon mines the flakes of it
                   heaped like snow, death-angel white
—poet journalist pioneer mother
uncovering her country:    *there are roads to take*

———————

I don't want to know how he tracked them
along the Appalachian Trail, hid close
by their tent, pitched as they thought in seclusion
killing one woman, the other
dragging herself into town    his defense they had teased his
                   loathing
of what they were    I don't want to know
but this is not a bad dream of mine    these are the materials
and so are the smell of wild mint and coursing water remembered
and the sweet salt darkred tissue I lay my face
upon, my tongue within.
                         A crosshair against the pupil of an eye
could blow my life from hers
a cell dividing without maps, sliver of ice beneath a wheel
could do the job.    Faithfulness isn't the problem.
          •

VII    (The dream-site)


Some rooftop, water-tank looming, street-racket strangely quelled
and others known and unknown there, long sweet summer eve-
              ning on the tarred roof:
leaned back your head to the nightvault swarming with stars
the Pleiades broken loose, not seven but thousands
every known constellation flinging out fiery threads
and you could distinguish all
—cobwebs, tendrils, anatomies of stars
coherently hammocked, blueblack avenues between
—you knew your way among them, knew you were part of them
until, neck aching, you sat straight up and saw:

It was New York, the dream-site
the lost city the city of dreadful light
where once as the sacks of garbage rose
like barricades around us we
stood listening to riffs from Pharaoh Sanders' window
on the brownstone steps
went striding the avenues in our fiery hair
in our bodies young and ordinary riding the subways reading
or pressed against other bodies
feeling in them the maps of Brooklyn Queens Manhattan
The Bronx unscrolling in the long breakneck
express plunges
                  as darkly we felt our own blood
streaming    a living city overhead
coherently webbed and knotted    bristling
we and all the others
                  known and unknown
living its life


VIII


He thought there would be a limit and that it would stop him.
          He depended on that:
        •

the cuts would be made by someone else, the direction
come from somewhere else, arrows flashing on the freeway.
That he'd end somewhere gazing
straight into It was what he imagined and nothing beyond.
That he'd end facing as limit a thing without limits and so he
         flung
and burned and hacked and bled himself toward that (if I
         understand
this story at all). What he found: FOR SALE: DO NOT
         DISTURB
OCCUPANT on some cliffs;   some ill-marked, ill-kept roads
ending in warnings about shellfish in Vietnamese, Spanish and
         English.
But the spray was any color he could have dreamed
—gold, ash, azure, smoke, moonstone—
and from time to time the ocean swirled up through the eye of a
         rock and taught him
limits.   Throwing itself backward, singing and sucking, no
         teacher, only its violent
self, the Pacific, dialectical waters rearing
their wild calm constructs, momentary, ancient.

---

If your voice could overwhelm those waters, what would it say?
What would it cry of the child swept under, the mother
on the beach then, in her black bathing suit, walking straight
         out
into the glazed lace as if she never noticed, what would it say of
         the father
facing inland in his shoes and socks at the edge of the tide,
what of the lost necklace glittering twisted in foam?
If your voice could crack in the wind hold its breath still as the
         rocks
what would it say to the daughter searching the tidelines for a
         bottled message
from the sunken slaveships?   what of the huge sun slowly defaulting into
         the clouds
what of the picnic stored in the dunes at high tide, full of the
    •

moon, the basket
with sandwiches, eggs, paper napkins, can-opener, the meal
packed for a family feast, excavated now by scuttling
ants, sandcrabs, dune-rats, because no one understood
all picnics are eaten on the grave?


IX


On this earth, in this life, as I read your story, you're lonely.
Lonely in the bar, on the shore of the coastal river
with your best friend, his wife, and your wife, fishing
lonely in the prairie classroom with all the students who love
                  you. You know some ghosts
come everywhere with you yet leave them unaddressed
for years.    You spend weeks in a house
with a drunk, you sober, whom you love, feeling lonely.
You grieve in loneliness, and if I understand you fuck in
                  loneliness.

I wonder if this is a white man's madness.
I honor your truth and refuse to leave it at that.

What have I learned from stories of the hunt, of lonely men in
                  gangs?
But there were other stories:
one man riding the Mohave Desert
another man walking the Grand Canyon.
I thought those solitary men were happy, as ever they had been.

Indio's long avenues
of Medjool date-palm and lemon sweep to the Salton Sea
in Yucca Flats the high desert reaches higher, bleached and spare
                  of talk.
At Twentynine Palms I found the grave
of Maria Eleanor Whallon, eighteen years, dead at the watering-
                  hole in 1903, under the now fire-branded palms
Her mother travelled on alone to cook in the mining camps.
        •

X

*Soledad.* = f. *Solitude, loneliness, homesickness, lonely retreat.*
Winter sun in the rosetrees.
An old Mexican with a white moustache prunes them back,
          spraying
the cut branches with dormant oil.    The old paper-bag-brown
          adobe walls
stretch apart from the rebuilt mission, in their own time.    It is
          lonely here
in the curve of the road winding through vast brown fields
          machine-engraved in furrows
of relentless precision.    In the small chapel
*Nuestra Señora de la Soledad* dwells in her shallow arch
painted on either side with columns.    She is in black lace crisp
          as cinders
from head to foot.    Alone, solitary, homesick
in her lonely retreat.    Outside black olives fall and smash
littering and staining the beaten path.    The gravestones of the
          padres
are weights pressing down on the Indian artisans.    It is the sixth
          day of another war.

          ——————————

Across the freeway stands another structure
from the other side of the mirror    *it destroys*
*the logical processes of the mind, a man's thoughts*
*become completely disorganized, madness streaming from every throat*
*frustrated sounds from the bars, metallic sounds from the walls*
*the steel trays, iron beds bolted to the wall, the smells, the human waste.*
*To determine how men will behave once they enter prison*
*it is of first importance to know that prison.*    (From the freeway
gun-turrets planted like water-towers in another garden, out-
          buildings spaced in winter sun
and the concrete mass beyond:    who now writes letters deep in-
          side that cave?)

*If my instructor tells me that the world and its affairs*
*are run as well as they possibly can be, that I am governed*
          •

*by wise and judicious men, that I am free and should be happy,*
*and if when I leave the instructor's presence and encounter*
*the exact opposite, if I actually sense or see confusion, war,*
*recession, depression, death and decay, is it not reasonable*
*that I should become perplexed?*
                                   From eighteen to twenty-eight
                                        of his years
a young man schools himself, argues,
debates, trains, lectures to himself,
teaches himself Swahili, Spanish, learns
five new words of English every day,
chainsmokes, reads, writes letters.
In this college of force he wrestles bitterness,
self-hatred, sexual anger, cures his own nature.
Seven of these years in solitary.    Soledad.

*But the significant feature of the desperate man reveals itself*
*when he meets other desperate men, directly or vicariously;*
*and he experiences his first kindness, someone to strain with him,*
*to strain to see him as he strains to see himself,*
*someone to understand, someone to accept the regard,*
*the love, that desperation forces into hiding.*
*Those feelings that find no expression in desperate times*
*store themselves up in great abundance, ripen, strengthen,*
*and strain the walls of their repository to the utmost;*
*where the kindred spirit touches this wall it crumbles—*
*no one responds to kindness, no one is more sensitive to it*
*than the desperate man.*

## XI

One night on Monterey Bay the death-freeze of the century:
a precise, detached calliper-grip holds the stars and quarter-
              moon
in arrest:    the hardiest plants crouch shrunken, a "killing frost"
on bougainvillea, Pride of Madeira, roseate black-purple succu-
              lents bowed
    •

juices sucked awry in one orgy of freezing
slumped on their stems like old faces evicted from cheap hotels
—*into the streets of the universe, now!*

Earthquake and drought followed by freezing followed by war.
Flags are blossoming now where little else is blossoming
and I am bent on fathoming what it means to love my country.
The history of this earth and the bones within it?
Soils and cities, promises made and mocked, plowed contours of
          shame and of hope?
Loyalties, symbols, murmurs extinguished and echoing?
Grids of states stretching westward, underground waters?
Minerals, traces, rumors I am made from, morsel, minuscule
          fibre, one woman
like and unlike so many, fooled as to her destiny, the scope of
          her task?
One citizen like and unlike so many, touched and untouched in
          passing
—each of us now a driven grain, a nucleus, a city in crisis
some busy constructing enclosures, bunkers, to escape the com-
          mon fate
some trying to revive dead statues to lead us, breathing their
          breath against marble lips
some who try to teach the moment, some who preach the
          moment
some who aggrandize, some who diminish themselves in the face
          of half-grasped events
—power and powerlessness run amuck, a tape reeling backward
          in jeering, screeching syllables—
some for whom war is new, others for whom it merely continues
          the old paroxysms of time
some marching for peace who for twenty years did not march for
          justice
some for whom peace is a white man's word and a white man's
          privilege
some who have learned to handle and contemplate the shapes of
          powerlessness and power
as the nurse learns hip and thigh and weight of the body he has
     •

to lift and sponge, day upon day
as she blows with her every skill on the spirit's embers still burn-
ing by their own laws in the bed of death.
A patriot is not a weapon.   A patriot is one who wrestles for the
soul of her country
as she wrestles for her own being, for the soul of his country
(gazing through the great circle at Window Rock into the sheen
of the Viet Nam Wall)
as he wrestles for his own being.   A patriot is a citizen trying to
wake
from the burnt-out dream of innocence, the nightmare
of the white general and the Black general posed in their
camouflage,
to remember her true country, remember his suffering land:
remember
that blessing and cursing are born as twins and separated at birth
to meet again in mourning
that the internal emigrant is the most homesick of all women and
of all men
that every flag that flies today is a cry of pain.
Where are we moored?
What are the bindings?
What behooves us?


XIII    (Dedications)

I know you are reading this poem
late, before leaving your office
of the one intense yellow lamp-spot and the darkening window
in the lassitude of a building faded to quiet
long after rush-hour.   I know you are reading this poem
standing up in a bookstore far from the ocean
on a grey day of early spring, faint flakes driven
across the plains' enormous spaces around you.
I know you are reading this poem
in a room where too much has happened for you to bear
where the bedclothes lie in stagnant coils on the bed
    •

and the open valise speaks of flight
but you cannot leave yet.    I know you are reading this poem
as the underground train loses momentum and before running
                        up the stairs
toward a new kind of love
your life has never allowed.
I know you are reading this poem by the light
of the television screen where soundless images jerk and slide
while you wait for the newscast from the *intifada.*
I know you are reading this poem in a waiting-room
of eyes met and unmeeting, of identity with strangers.
I know you are reading this poem by fluorescent light
in the boredom and fatigue of the young who are counted out,
count themselves out, at too early an age.    I know
you are reading this poem through your failing sight, the thick
lens enlarging these letters beyond all meaning yet you read on
because even the alphabet is precious.
I know you are reading this poem as you pace beside the stove
warming milk, a crying child on your shoulder, a book in your
                        hand
because life is short and you too are thirsty.
I know you are reading this poem which is not in your language
guessing at some words while others keep you reading
and I want to know which words they are.
I know you are reading this poem listening for something, torn
                        between bitterness and hope
turning back once again to the task you cannot refuse.
I know you are reading this poem because there is nothing
                        else left to read
there where you have landed, stripped as you are.

1990–1991

# That Mouth

This is the girl's mouth, the taste
daughters, not sons, obtain:
These are the lips, powerful rudders
pushing through groves of kelp,
the girl's terrible, unsweetened taste
of the whole ocean, its fathoms: this is that taste.

This is not the father's kiss, the mother's:
a father can try to choke you,
a mother drown you to save you:
all the transactions have long been enacted.
This is neither a sister's tale nor a brother's:
strange trade-offs have long been made.

This is the swallow, the splash
of krill and plankton, that mouth
described as a girl's—
enough to give you a taste:
Are you a daughter, are you a son?
Strange trade-offs have long been made.

1988

# Marghanita

at the oak table under the ceiling fan
Marghanita at the table counting up
a dead woman's debts.
                    •

Kicks off a sandal, sips
soda from a can, wedges the last bills
under the candelabrum.     She is here
because no one else was there when worn-to-skeleton
her enemy died.     Her love.     Her twin.
Marghanita dreamed the intravenous, the intensive
the stainless steel
before she ever saw them.     She's not practical,
you know, they used to say.
She's the artist, she got away.

In her own place Marghanita glues bronze
feathers into wings, smashes green and clear
bottles into bloodletting particles
crushed into templates of sand
scores mirrors till they fall apart and sticks them up
in driftwood boughs, drinks golden
liquid with a worm's name, forgets
her main enemy, her twin;
scores her wrist on a birthday
dreams the hospital dream.

When they were girl and boy together, boy and girl
she pinned his arm against his back
for a box containing false
lashes and fingernails, a set of veils, a string of pearls,
she let go and listened to his tales
she breathed their breath, he hers,
they each had names only the other knew.

Marghanita in the apartment everyone has left:
not a nephew, not a niece,
nobody from the parish
—gone into hiding, emigrated, lost?
where are the others?
Marghanita comes back because she does,
adding up what's left:
a rainsoaked checkbook, snapshots
     •

razed from an album,
colors ground into powder, brushes, wands
for eyelids, lashes, brows,
beads of bath-oil, tubes of glycerin
—a dead woman's luxuries.

Marghanita will
take care of it all.　Pay if nothing else
the last month's rent.　The wings of the fan
stir corners of loose paper,
light ebbs from the window-lace,
she needs to go out and eat.　And so
hating and loving come down
to a few columns of figures,
an aching stomach, a care taken:　something done.

1989


# Tattered Kaddish

Taurean reaper of the wild apple field
messenger from earthmire gleaning
transcripts of fog
in the nineteenth year and the eleventh month
speak your tattered Kaddish for all suicides:

Praise to life though it crumbled in like a tunnel
on ones we knew and loved

　　Praise to life though its windows blew shut
　　on the breathing-room of ones we knew and loved

Praise to life though ones we knew and loved
loved it badly, too well, and not enough
　　•

Praise to life though it tightened like a knot
on the hearts of ones we thought we knew loved us

Praise to life giving room and reason
to ones we knew and loved who felt unpraisable

Praise to them, how they loved it, when they could.

1989


# Final Notations


it will not be simple, it will not be long
it will take little time, it will take all your thought
it will take all your heart, it will take all your breath
it will be short, it will not be simple

it will touch through your ribs, it will take all your heart
it will not be long, it will occupy your thought
as a city is occupied, as a bed is occupied
it will take all your flesh, it will not be simple

You are coming into us who cannot withstand you
you are coming into us who never wanted to withstand you
you are taking parts of us into places never planned
you are going far away with pieces of our lives

it will be short, it will take all your breath
it will not be simple, it will become your will

1991

From

*Dark Fields of
the Republic*

1995

# What Kind of Times Are These

There's a place between two stands of trees where the grass grows
        uphill
and the old revolutionary road breaks off into shadows
near a meeting-house abandoned by the persecuted
who disappeared into those shadows.

I've walked there picking mushrooms at the edge of dread, but
        don't be fooled,
this isn't a Russian poem, this is not somewhere else but here,
our country moving closer to its own truth and dread,
its own ways of making people disappear.

I won't tell you where the place is, the dark mesh of the woods
meeting the unmarked strip of light—
ghost-ridden crossroads, leafmold paradise:
I know already who wants to buy it, sell it, make it disappear.

And I won't tell you where it is, so why do I tell you
anything? Because you still listen, because in times like these
to have you listen at all, it's necessary
to talk about trees.

1991

# In Those Years

In those years, people will say, we lost track
of the meaning of *we,* of *you*
we found ourselves
   •

reduced to *I*
and the whole thing became
silly, ironic, terrible:
we were trying to live a personal life
and, yes, that was the only life
we could bear witness to

But the great dark birds of history screamed and plunged
into our personal weather
They were headed somewhere else but their beaks and pinions drove
along the shore, through the rags of fog
where we stood, saying *I*

1991


# Calle Visión

*1*

Not what you thought:    just a turn-off
leading downhill not up

narrow, doesn't waste itself
has a house at the far end

scrub oak and cactus in the yard
some cats    some snakes

in the house there is a room
in the room there is a bed

on the bed there is a blanket
that tells the coming of the railroad
              •

under the blanket there are sheets
scrubbed transparent here and there

under the sheets there's a mattress
the old rough kind, with buttons and ticking

under the mattress is a frame
of rusting iron   still strong

the whole bed smells of soap and rust
the window smells of old tobacco-dust and rain

this is your room
in Calle Visión

if you took the turn-off
it was for you

2

Calle Visión   sand in your teeth
granules of cartilage in your wrists

Calle Visión   firestorm behind
shuttered eyelids   fire in your foot

Calle Visión   rocking the gates
of your locked bones

Calle Visión   dreamnet dropped
over your porous sleep

3

Lodged in the difficult hotel
all help withheld
    •

*a place not to live but to die in*
*not an inn but a hospital*

a friend's love came to me
touched and took me away

in a car    love
of a curmudgeon, a short-fuse

and as he drove    eyes on the road
I felt his love

and that was simply the case    the way things were
unstated and apparent

and like the rest of it
clear as a dream


4

Calle Visión    your heart beats on unbroken
    how is this possible

Calle Visión    wounded knee
    wounded spine    wounded eye

        *Have you ever worked around metal?*
        *Are there particles under your skin?*

Calle Visión    but your heart is still whole
    how is this possible

since what can be    will be taken
    when not offered in trust and faith

by the collectors of collectibles
    the professors of what-has-been-suffered
        •

*The world is falling down   hold my hand*
*It's a lonely sound   hold my hand*

Calle Visión    never forget
    the body's pain

never divide it

5

Ammonia
        carbon dioxide
                carbon monoxide
                            methane
                    hydrogen sulfide
:   the gasses that rise from urine and feces

in the pig confinement units known as nurseries
can eat a metal doorknob off in half a year

pig-dander
        dust from dry manure
—lung-scar:    breath-shortedness an early symptom

*And the fire shall try*
*every man's work*   :Calle Visión:
and every woman's

if you took the turn-off
this is your revelation   this the source

6

The repetitive motions of slaughtering
        —fire in wrists   in elbows—
the dead birds coming at you along the line
        —how you smell them in your sleep—
        •

fire in your wrist    blood packed
    under your fingernails   heavy air
doors padlocked on the outside
    —you might steal a chicken—
fire in the chicken factory fire
    in the carpal tunnel   leaping the frying vats
yellow smoke from soybean oil
    and wasted parts and insulating wire
—some fleeing to the freezer some
    found "stuck in poses of escape"—


7


You can call on beauty still and it will leap
from all directions

you can write beauty into the cruel file
of things done    things left undone    but

once we were dissimilar
yet unseparate    that's beauty    that's what you catch

in the newborn's midnight gaze
the fog that melts the falling stars

the virus from the smashed lianas driven
searching now for us


8


In the room    in the house
in Calle Visión

all you want    is to lie down
alone on your back    let your hands

slide lightly over your hipbones
But she's there with her remnants her cross-sections
    •

trying to distract you
with her childhood her recipes her

cargo of charred pages her
carved and freckled neck-stones

her crying-out-for-witness her
backward-forward timescapes

her suitcase in Berlin
and the one lost and found

in her island go-and-come
—is she terrified you will forget her?

9

In the black net
of her orange wing

the angry nightblown butterfly
hangs on a piece of lilac in the sun

carried overland like her
from a long way off

She has travelled hard and far
and her interrogation goes:

*—Hands dripping with wet earth*
*head full of shocking dreams*

*O what have you buried all these years*
*what have you dug up?*
          •

This place is alive with the dead and with the living
I have never been alone here

I wear my triple eye as I walk along the road
past, present, future all are at my side

Storm-beaten, tough-winged passenger
there is nothing I have buried that can die

*10*

On the road there is a house
scrub oak and cactus in the yard

lilac carried overland
from a long way off

in the house there is a bed
on the bed there is a blanket

telling the coming of the railroad
under the mattress there's a frame

of rusting iron    still strong
the window smells of old tobacco-dust and rain

the window smells of old
tobacco-dust and rain

1992–1993

# Then or Now

*Is it necessary for me to write obliquely*
*about the situation? Is that what*
*you would have me do?*

*FOOD PACKAGES: 1947*

Powdered milk, chocolate bars, canned fruit, tea,
salamis, aspirin:
Four packages a month to her old professor in Heidelberg
and his Jewish wife:
Europe is trying to revive an intellectual life
and the widow of the great sociologist needs flour.

Europe is trying/to revive/
with the Jews somewhere else.

The young ex-philosopher tries to feed her teachers
all the way from New York, with orders for butter from Denmark,
sending dispatches into the fog
of the European spirit:
*I am no longer German. I am a Jew and the German language*
*was once my home.*

1993

*INNOCENCE: 1945*

"The beauty of it was the guilt.
It entered us, quick *schnapps,*
forked tongue of ice.   The guilt
    •

made us feel innocent again.
We had done nothing while some
extreme measures were taken.   We drifted.   In the
Snow Queen's huge ballrom had dreamed
of the whole world and a new pair of skates.
But we had suffered too.
The miracle was:   felt
nothing.   Felt we had done
nothing.   Nothing to do.   Felt free.
And we had suffered, too.
It was that freedom we craved,
cold needle in the bloodstream.
Guilt after all was a feeling."

1993


*SUNSET, DECEMBER, 1993*

Dangerous of course to draw
parallels   Yet more dangerous to write

as if there were a steady course, we and our poems
protected:   the individual life, protected

poems, ideas, gliding
in mid-air, innocent

I walked out on the deck and every board
was luminous with cold dew   It could freeze tonight

Each board is different of course but each does gleam
wet, under a complicated sky:   mounds of swollen ink

heavy gray unloading up the coast
a rainbow suddenly and casually

unfolding its span
Dangerous not to think

•

how the earth still was   in places
while the chimneys shuddered with the first dischargements

1993


*DEPORTATIONS*

It's happened already while we were still
searching for patterns   A turn of the head
toward a long horizontal window overlooking the city
to see people being taken
neighbors, vendors, paramedicals
hurried from their porches, their tomato stalls
their auto-mechanic arguments
and children from schoolyards
There are far more of the takers-away than the taken
at this point anyway

Then:   dream-cut:   our house:
four men walk through the unlatched door
One in light summer wool and silken tie
One in work clothes browned with blood
One with open shirt, a thin
thong necklace hasped with silver around his neck
One in shorts naked up from the navel

And they have come for us, two of us and four of them
and I think, perhaps they are still human
and I ask them   *When do you think all this began?*

as if trying to distract them from their purpose
as if trying to appeal to a common bond
as if one of them might be you
as if I were practicing for something
yet to come

1994

*AND NOW*

And now as you read these poems
—you whose eyes and hands I love
—you whose mouth and eyes I love
—you whose words and minds I love—
don't think I was trying to state a case
or construct a scenery:
I tried to listen to
the public voice of our time
tried to survey our public space
as best I could
—tried to remember and stay
faithful to details, note
precisely how the air moved
and where the clock's hands stood
and who was in charge of definitions
and who stood by receiving them
when the name of compassion
was changed to the name of guilt
when to feel with a human stranger
was declared obsolete.

1994

# Late Ghazal

Footsole to scalp alive facing the window's black mirror.
First rains of the winter    morning's smallest hour.

Go back to the ghazal then    what will you do there?
Life always pulsed harder than the lines.

Do you remember the strands that ran from eye to eye?
The tongue that reached everywhere, speaking all the parts?
          •

Everything there was cast in an image of desire.
The imagination's cry is a sexual cry.

I took my body anyplace with me.
In the thickets of abstraction my skin ran with blood.

Life was always stronger . . . the critics couldn't get it.
Memory says the music always ran ahead of the words.

1994


## *from* Inscriptions

*ONE: COMRADE*

Little as I knew you I know you:    little as you knew me you
          know me
—that's the light we stand under when we meet.
I've looked into flecked jaws
walked injured beaches footslick in oil
watching licked birds stumble in flight
while you drawn through the pupil of your eye
across your own oceans in visionary pain and in relief
headlong and by choice took on the work of charting
your city's wounds ancient and fertile
listening for voices within and against.
My testimony:    yours:    Trying to keep faith
not with each other exactly yet it's the one known and unknown
who stands for, imagines the other    with whom faith could
          be kept.

In city your mind burns wanes waxes with hope
(no stranger to bleakness you:    worms have toothed at
          your truths
but you were honest regarding that).
          •

You conspired to compile the illegal discography
of songs forbidden to sing or to be heard.
If there were ethical flowers one would surely be yours
and I'd hand it to you headlong across landmines
across city's whyless sleeplight I'd hand it
purposefully, with love, a hand trying to keep beauty afloat
on the bacterial waters.

When a voice learns to sing it can be heard as dangerous
when a voice learns to listen it can be heard as desperate.
The self unlocked to many selves.
A mirror handed to one who just released
from the locked ward from solitary from preventive detention
sees in her thicket of hair her lost eyebrows
whole populations.
One who discharged from war stares in the looking-glass of home
at what he finds there, sees in the undischarged tumult of his
            own eye
how thickskinned peace is, and those who claim to promote it.


*TWO: MOVEMENT*

Old backswitching road bent toward the ocean's light
Talking of angles of vision    movements    a black or a red tulip
            opening
Times of walking across a street    thinking
not *I have joined a movement* but    *I am stepping in this deep current*
*Part of my life washing behind me    terror I couldn't swim with*
*part of my life waiting for me    a part I had no words for*
*I need to live each day through    have them and know them all*
*though I can see from here where I'll be standing at the end.*

-------------

When does a life bend toward freedom?    grasp its direction?
How do you know you're not circling in pale dreams, nostalgia,
            stagnation
but entering that deep current    malachite, colorado
        •

requiring all your strength wherever found
your patience and your labor
desire pitted against desire's inversion
all your mind's fortitude?
Maybe through a teacher:    someone with facts with numbers
        with poetry
who wrote on the board:    IN EVERY GENERATION ACTION FREES
        OUR DREAMS.
Maybe a student:   one mind unfurling like a redblack peony
quenched into percentile, dropout, stubbed-out bud
—Your journals Patricia:   Douglas your poems:   but the repeti-
        tive blows
on spines whose hope you were, on yours:
to see that quenching and decide.

—And now she turns her face brightly on the new morning in
        the new classroom
new in her beauty her skin her lashes her lively body:
*Race, class . . . all that . . . but isn't all that just history?*
*Aren't people bored with it all?*

She could be
myself at nineteen   but free of reverence for past ideas
ignorant of hopes piled on her   She's a mermaid
momentarily precipitated from a solution
which could stop her heart   She could swim or sink
like a beautiful crystal.

## FOUR: HISTORY

Should I simplify my life for you?
Don't ask how I began to love men.
Don't ask how I began to love women.
Remember the forties songs, the slowdance numbers
the small sex-filled gas-rationed Chevrolet?
Remember walking in the snow and who was gay?
Cigarette smoke of the movies, silver-and-gray
    •

profiles, dreaming the dreams of he-and-she
breathing the dissolution of the wisping silver plume?
Dreaming that dream we leaned applying lipstick
by the gravestone's mirror when we found ourselves
playing in the cemetery.   In Current Events she said
the war in Europe is over, the Allies
and she wore no lipstick have won the war
and we raced screaming out of Sixth Period.

Dreaming that dream
we had to maze our ways through a wood
where lips were knives breasts razors and I hid
in the cage of my mind scribbling
*this map stops where it all begins*
into a red-and-black notebook.
Remember after the war when peace came down
as plenty for some and they said we were saved
in an eternal present and we knew the world could end?
—remember after the war when peace rained down
on the winds from Hiroshima Nagasaki Utah Nevada?
and the socialist queer Christian teacher jumps from the
        hotel window?
and L.G. saying *I want to sleep with you but not for sex*
and the red-and-black enamelled coffee-pot dripped slow through
        the dark grounds
—appetite terror power tenderness
the long kiss in the stairwell the switch thrown
on two Jewish Communists married to each other
the definitive crunch of glass at the end of the wedding?
*(When shall we learn, what should be clear as day,*
*We cannot choose what we are free to love?)*


*SIX: EDGELIT*


Living under fire in the raincolored opal of your love
I could have forgotten other women I desired
so much I wanted to love them but
here are some reasons love would not let me:
      •

One had a trick of dropping her lashes along her cheekbone
in an amazing screen so she saw nothing.
Another would stand in summer arms rounded and warm
catching wild apricots that fell
either side of a broken fence but she caught them on one
        side only.
One, ambitious, flushed
to the collarbone, a shapely coward.
One keen as mica, glittering,
full at the lips, absent at the core.
One who flirted with danger
had her escape route planned when others had none
and disappeared.
One sleepwalking on the trestle
of privilege dreaming of innocence
tossing her cigarette into the dry gully
—an innocent gesture.

---

Medbh's postcard from Belfast:
                      *one's poetry seems aimless*
*covered in the blood and lies*
                      *oozing corrupt & artificial*
*but of course one will continue . . .*

This week I've dredged my pages
for anything usable
                  head, heart, perforated
by raw disgust and fear
If I dredge up anything it's suffused
by what it works in, "like the dyer's hand"
I name it unsteady, slick, unworthy
                     and I go on

In my sixty-fifth year I know something about language:
it can eat or be eaten by experience
Medbh, poetry means refusing
the choice to kill or die
     •

but this life of continuing is for the sane mad
and the bravest monsters

———————————

The bright planet that plies her crescent shape
in the western air   that through the screendoor gazes
with her curved eye now speaks:   *The beauty of darkness
is how it lets you see.*   Through the screendoor
she told me this and half-awake I scrawled
her words on a piece of paper.
She is called Venus but I call her You
You   who sees me   You   who calls me to see
You   who has other errands far away in space and time
You   in your fiery skin   acetylene
scorching the claims of the false mystics
You   who like the moon arrives in crescent
changeable changer   speaking truth from darkness

———————————

Edgelit:   firegreen yucca under fire-ribbed clouds
blue-green agave   grown huge in flower
cries of birds streaming over

The night of the eclipse the full
moon
swims clear between flying clouds until

the hour of the occlusion   It's not of aging
anymore and its desire
which is of course unending

it's of dying   young or old
in full desire

*Remember me . . . . O, O, O,
O, remember me*

*these vivid stricken cells
precarious living marrow*

•

*this my labyrinthine filmic brain*
*this my dreaded blood*
*this my irreplaceable*
*footprint vanishing from the air*

dying in full desire
thirsting for the coldest water
hungering for hottest food
gazing into the wildest light

edgelight from the high desert
where shadows drip from tiniest stones
sunklight of bloody afterglow

torque of the Joshua tree
flinging itself forth in winter
factoring freeze into its liquid consciousness

These are the extremes I stoke
into the updraft of this life
still roaring

                into thinnest air

1993–1994

From

*Midnight Salvage*

1999

# For an Anniversary

The wing of the osprey lifted
over the nest on Tomales Bay
into fog and difficult gust
raking treetops from Inverness Ridge on over
The left wing shouldered into protective
gesture the left wing we thought broken

and the young beneath in the windy nest
creaking there in their hunger
and the tides beseeching, besieging
the bay in its ruined languor

1996


# Midnight Salvage

1

Up skyward through a glazed rectangle I
sought the light of a so-called heavenly body
: : a planet or our moon in some event and caught

nothing nothing but a late wind
pushing around some Monterey pines
themselves in trouble and rust-limbed

Nine o'clock : : July : the light
undrained : : that blotted blue
that lets has let will let
                •

thought's blood ebb between life- and death-time
darkred behind darkblue
bad news pulsing back and forth of "us" and "them"

And all I wanted was to find an old
friend an old figure an old trigonometry
still true to our story in orbits flaming or cold


2


Under the conditions of my hiring
I could profess or declare anything at all
since in that place nothing would change
So many fountains, such guitars at sunset

Did not want any more to sit under such a window's
deep embrasure, wisteria bulging on spring air
in that borrowed chair
with its collegiate shield at a borrowed desk

under photographs of the spanish steps, Keats' death mask
and the english cemetery all so under control and so eternal
in burnished frames : : or occupy the office
of the marxist-on-sabbatical

with Gramsci's fast-fading eyes
thumbtacked on one wall opposite a fading print
of the same cemetery : : had memories
and death masks of my own : : could not any more

peruse young faces already straining for
the production of slender testaments
to swift reading and current thinking : : would not wait
for the stroke of noon to declare all passions obsolete

Could not play by the rules
in that palmy place : : nor stand at lectern professing
                •

anything at all
                    in their hire


3

Had never expected hope would form itself
completely in my time : : was never so sanguine
as to believe old injuries could transmute easily
through any singular event or idea : : never
so feckless as to ignore the managed contagion
of ignorance the contrived discontinuities
the felling of leaders and future leaders
the pathetic erections of soothsayers

But thought I was conspiring, breathing-along
with history's systole-diastole
twenty thousand leagues under the sea a mammal heartbeat
sheltering another heartbeat
plunging from the Farallons all the way to Baja
sending up here or there a blowhole signal
and sometimes beached
making for warmer waters
where the new would be delivered : : though I would not see it


4

But neither was expecting in my time
to witness this : : wasn't deep
lucid or mindful you might say enough
to look through history's bloodshot eyes
into this commerce this dreadnought wreck cut loose
from all vows, oaths, patents, compacts, promises : :
                                        To see
not O my Captain
fallen cold & dead by the assassin's hand

but cold alive & cringing : : drinking with the assassins
        •

in suit of noir Hong Kong silk
pushing his daughter in her famine-
waisted flamingo gown
out on the dance floor with the traffickers
in nerve gas saying to them *Go for it*
and to the girl *Get with it*


5


When I ate and drank liberation once I walked
arm-in-arm with someone who said she had something to teach me
It was the avenue and the dwellers
free of home : roofless : : women
without pots to scour or beds to make
or combs to run through hair
or hot water for lifting grease or cans
to open or soap to slip in that way
under arms then beneath breasts then downward to thighs

Oil-drums were alight under the freeway
and bottles reached from pallets of cardboard corrugate
and piles of lost and found to be traded back and forth
and figures arranging themselves from the wind
Through all this she walked me : : And said
My name is Liberation and I come from here
Of what are you so afraid?

We've hung late in the bars like bats
kissed goodnight at the stoplights
—did you think I wore this city without pain?
did you think I had no family?


6


Past the curve where the old craftsman was run down
there's a yard called Midnight Salvage
He was walking in the road which was always safe
            •

The young driver did not know that road
its curves or that people walked there
or that you could speed yet hold the curve
watching for those who walked there
such skills he did not have being in life unpracticed

but I have driven that road in madness and driving rain
thirty years in love and pleasure and grief-blind
on ice I have driven it and in the vague haze of summer
between clumps of daisies and sting of fresh cowflop odors
lucky I am I hit nobody old or young
killed nobody left no trace
practiced in life as I am

7

This horrible patience which is part of the work
This patience which waits for language for meaning for the
        least sign
This encumbered plodding state doggedly dragging
the IV up and down the corridor
with the plastic sack of bloodstained urine

Only so can you start living again
waking to take the temperature of the soul
when the black irises lean at dawn
from the mouth of the bedside pitcher
This condition in which you swear *I will*
*submit to whatever poetry is*
*I accept no limits*    Horrible patience

8

You cannot eat an egg    You don't know where it's been
The ordinary body of the hen
vouchsafes no safety    The countryside refuses to supply
Milk is powdered    meat's in both senses high
    •

Old walls the pride of architects   collapsing
find us in crazed niches   sleeping like foxes
we wanters we unwanted we
wanted for the crime of being ourselves

Fame slides on its belly like any other animal after food
Ruins are disruptions of system leaking in
weeds and light   redrawing
the City of Expectations

You cannot eat an egg   Unstupefied not unhappy
we braise wild greens and garlic   feed the feral cats
and when the fog's irregular documents break open
scan its fissures for young stars
                    in the belt of Orion

1996


# Char

1

There is bracken there is the dark mulberry
there is the village where no villager survived
there are the hitlerians there are the foresters
feeding the partisans from frugal larders

there is the moon ablaze in every quarter
there is the moon "of tin and sage" and unseen pilots dropping
explosive gifts into meadows of fog and crickets
there is the cuckoo and the tiny snake
            •

there is the table set at every meal
for freedom whose chair stays vacant
the young men in their newfound passions
*(Love along with them the ones they love)*

Obscurity, code, the invisible existence
of a thrush in the reeds, the poet watching
as the blood washes off the revolver in the bucket
*Redbreast, your song shakes loose a ruin of memories*

*A horrible day . . . Perhaps he knew, at that final instant?*
*The village had to be spared at any price . . .*
*How can you hear me? I speak from so far . . .*
*The flowering broom hid us in a blazing yellow mist . . .*

2

*This war will prolong itself beyond any platonic armistice. The implanting*
*of political concepts will go on amid upheavals and under cover of*
*self-confident hypocrisy. Don't smile. Thrust aside both skepticism and res-*
*ignation and prepare your soul to face an intramural confrontation with*
*demons as cold-blooded as microbes.*

The poet in wartime, the Surréalistes' younger brother
turned realist *(the village had to be spared at any price)*
all eyes on him in the woods crammed with maquisards expecting him to
signal to fire and save their comrade
shook his head and watched Bernard's execution
knowing that *the random shooting of a revolver*
may be *the simplest surreal act* but never
changes the balance of power and that real acts are not simple
*The poet, prone to exaggerate, thinks clearly under torture*

knowing the end of the war
would mean no end to the microbes frozen in each soul
the young freedom fighters
in love with the Resistance
   •

fed by a thrill for violence
familiar as his own jaw under the razor

3

Insoluble riverrain conscience echo of the future
I keep vigil for you here by the reeds of Elkhorn Slough
and the brown mouth of the Salinas River going green
where the white egret fishes the fragile margins
Hermetic guide in resistance I've found you and lost you
several times in my life   You were never just
the poet appalled and transfixed by war you were the maker
of terrible delicate decisions and that did not smudge
your sense of limits   You saw squirrels crashing
from the tops of burning pines when the canister exploded
and worse and worse and you were in charge of every risk
the incendiary motives of others were in your charge
and the need for a courage wrapped in absolute tact
and you decided and lived like that and you
held poetry at your lips a piece of wild thyme ripped
from a burning meadow a mimosa twig
from still unravaged country   You kept your senses
about you like that and like this I keep vigil for you.

1996

# Letters to a Young Poet

1

Your photograph won't do you justice
those wetted anthill mounds won't let you focus
that lens on the wetlands
     &bull;

five swans chanting overhead
distract your thirst for closure
and quick escape

2

Let me turn you around in your frozen nightgown and say
one word to you: Ineluctable

—meaning, you won't get quit
of this: the worst of the new news

history running back and forth
panic in the labyrinth

—I will not touch you further:
your choice to freeze or not

to say, you and I are caught in
a laboratory without a science

3

Would it gladden you to think
poetry could purely

take its place beneath lightning sheets
or fogdrip   live its own life

screamed at, howled down
by a torn bowel of dripping names

—composers visit Terezin, film-makers Sarajevo
Cabrini-Green or Edenwald Houses

   ineluctable
      •

if a woman as vivid as any artist
can fling any day herself from the 14th floor

would it relieve you to decide    *Poetry
doesn't make this happen?*


4

From the edges of your own distraction turn
the cloth-weave up, its undersea-fold venous

with sorrow's wash and suck, pull and release,
        annihilating rush

to and fro, fabric of caves, the onset of your fear
kicking away their lush and slippery flora nurseried
        in liquid glass

trying to stand fast in rootsuck, in distraction,
        trying to wade this
undertow of utter repetition

Look: with all my fear I'm here with you, trying what it
        means, to stand fast; what it means to move


5

Beneaped. Rowboat, pirogue, caught between the lowest
and highest tides of spring. Beneaped. Befallen,
becalmed, benighted, yes, begotten.
—*Be*—infernal prefix of the actionless.
—*Be*—as in Sit, Stand, Lie, Obey.
The dog's awful desire that takes his brain
and lays it at the boot-heel.

You can be like this forever—*Be*
as without movement.
        •

6

But this is how
I come, anyway, pushing up from below
my head wrapped in a chequered scarf a lanterned helmet on this
          head
pushing up out of the ore
this sheeted face this lanterned head facing the seep of death
my lips having swum through silt
     clearly pronouncing
Hello and farewell

Who, anyway, wants to know
this pale mouth, this stick
of crimson lipsalve Who my
dragqueen's vocal chords my bitter beat
my overshoulder backglance flung
at the great strophes and antistrophes
my chant my ululation my sacred parings
nails, hair my dysentery my hilarious throat

my penal colony's birdstarved ledge my face downtown
in films by Sappho and Artaud?

Everyone.    For a moment.


7

It's not the déjà vu that kills
it's the foreseeing
the head that speaks from the crater

I wanted to go somewhere
the brain had not yet gone
I wanted not to be
there so alone.

1997

# Camino Real

Hot stink of skunk
crushed at the vineyards' edge

hawk-skied, carrion-clean
clouds ranging themselves
over enormous autumn

that scribble   edged and skunky
as the great road winds on
toward my son's house seven hours south


Walls of the underpass
smudged and blistered eyes gazing from armpits
THE WANTER WANTED    ARMED IN LOVE AND
            DANGEROUS
WANTED FOR WANTING


To become the scholar of : :
: : to list compare contrast events to footnote lesser evils
calmly to note "bedsprings"
describe how they were wired
to which parts of the body

to make clear-eyed assessments of the burnt-out eye : : investigate
the mouth-bit and the mouth
the half-swole slippery flesh the enforced throat
the whip they played you with the backroad games the beatings by
            the river
                •

O to list collate commensurate to quantify:
*I was the one, I suffered, I was there*

never
to trust to memory only

to go back    notebook in hand
dressed as no one there was dressed

over and over to quantify
on a gridded notebook page

The difficulty of proving
such things were done for no reason
that every night
"in those years"
people invented reasons for torture

Asleep now,    head in hands
hands over ears    O you
Who do this work
every one of you
every night

Driving south:    santabarbara's barbarous
landscaped mind:    lest it be forgotten
in the long sweep downcoast

let it not be exonerated

but O the light
on the raw Pacific silks

Charles Olson:    "Can you afford not to make
                        the magical study
                            which happiness is?"

•

I take him to mean
that happiness is in itself a magical study
a glimpse of the *unhandicapped life*
as it might be for anyone, somewhere

a kind of alchemy, a study of transformation
else it withers, wilts

—that happiness is not to be
mistrusted or wasted
though it ferment in grief

George Oppen to June Degnan:    "I don't know how
to measure happiness"
—Why measure? in itself it's the measure—

at the end of a day
        of great happiness if there be such a day

drawn by love's unprovable pull

I write this, sign it
                        Adrienne

1997


# Seven Skins

1

Walk along back of the library
in 1952
someone's there to catch your eye
Vic Greenberg in his wheelchair
        •

paraplegic GI—
Bill of Rights Jew
graduate student going in
by the only elevator route
up into the great stacks where
all knowledge should and is
and shall be stored like sacred grain
while the loneliest of lonely
American decades goes aground
on the postwar rock
and some unlikely
shipmates found ourselves
stuck amid so many smiles

Dating Vic Greenberg you date
crutches and a chair
a cool wit an outrageous form:
"—just back from a paraplegics' conference,
guess what the biggest meeting was about—
Sex with a Paraplegic!—for the wives—"
In and out of cabs his chair
opening and closing round his
electrical monologue the air
furiously calm around him
as he transfers to the crutches

But first you go for cocktails
in his room at Harvard
he mixes the usual martinis, plays Billie Holiday
talks about Melville's vision of evil
and the question of the postwar moment:
Is there an American civilization?
In the bathroom huge
grips and suction-cupped
rubber mats long-handled sponges
the reaching tools a veteran's benefits
in plainest sight
.

And this is only memory, no more
so this is how you remember

Vic Greenberg takes you to the best restaurant
which happens to have no stairs
for talk about movies, professors, food
Vic orders wine and tastes it
you have lobster, he Beef Wellington
the famous dessert is baked alaska
ice cream singed in a flowerpot
from the oven, a live tulip inserted there

Chair to crutches, crutches to cab
chair in the cab and back to Cambridge
memory shooting its handheld frames
Shall I drop you, he says, or shall
we go back to the room for a drink?
It's the usual question
a man has to ask it
a woman has to answer
you don't even think

2

What a girl I was then what a body
ready for breaking open like a lobster
what a little provincial village
what a hermit crab seeking nobler shells
what a beach of rattling stones what an offshore raincloud
what a gone-and-come tidepool

what a look into eternity I took and did not return it
what a book I made myself
what a quicksilver study
bright little bloodstain
liquid pouches escaping
        •

What a girl pelican-skimming over fear what a mica lump
        splitting
into tiny sharp-edged mirrors through which
the sun's eclipse could seem normal
what a sac of eggs what a drifting flask
eager to sink   to be found
to disembody   what a mass of swimmy legs


3


Vic into what shoulder could I have pushed your face
laying hands first on your head
onto whose thighs pulled down your head
which fear of mine would have wound itself
around which of yours   could we have taken it   nakedness
without sperm   in what insurrectionary
convulsion would we have done it   mouth to mouth
mouth-tongue to vulva-tongue to anus   earlobe to nipple
what seven skins each have to molt what seven shifts
what tears boil up through sweat to bathe
what humiliatoriums   what layers of imposture

What heroic tremor
released into pure moisture
might have soaked our shape   two-headed   avid
into your heretic
linen-service
sheets?


1997

# Rusted Legacy

Imagine a city where nothing's
forgiven   your deed adheres
to you like a scar, a tattoo    but almost everything's
forgotten    deer flattened leaping a highway for food
the precise reason for the shaving of the confused girl's head
the small boys' punishing of the frogs
—a city memory-starved but intent on retributions
Imagine the architecture   the governance
the men and the women in power
—tell me if it is not true you still
          live in that city.

Imagine a city partitioned    divorced from its hills
where temples and telescopes used to probe the stormy codices
a city brailling through fog
thicket and twisted wire
into dark's velvet dialectic
sewers which are also rivers
art's unchartered aquifers    the springhead
sprung open in civic gardens left unlocked at night
I finger the glass beads I strung and wore
under the pines while the arrests were going on
(transfixed from neck to groin I wanted to save what I could)
They brought trays with little glasses of cold water
into the dark park   a final village gesture
before the villages were gutted.
They were trying to save what they could
—tell me if this is not the same city.

I have forced myself to come back like a daughter
required to put her mother's house in order
whose hands need terrible gloves to handle
          •

the medicinals    the disease packed in those linens
Accomplished criminal I've been but
can I accomplish justice here? Tear the old wedding sheets
into cleaning rags? Faithless daughter
like stone    but with water pleating across
Let water be water let stone be stone
Tell me is this the same city.

This *I*—must she, must she lie scabbed with rust
crammed with memory in a place
of little anecdotes    no one left
to go around gathering the full dissident story?
Rusting her hands and shoulders stone her lips
yet leaching down from her eyesockets tears
—for one self only? each encysts a city.

1997

# From

## *Fox*

2001

# Veterans Day

1

No flag heavy or full enough to hide this face
this body swung home from home    sewn into its skin

Let you    entrusted to close the box
for final draping    take care

what might be due
to the citizen wounded

by no foreign blast nor shell    *(is this*
*body a child's?    if?    why?)*

eyes hooded in refusal—
over these to lower the nation's pall, thick flutter

this body shriveled into itself
—a normal process they have said

The face?    another story, a flag
hung upside down against glory's orders


2

Trying to think about
something else—what?—when

*the story broke*
the scissor-fingered prestidigitators
                •

snipped the links of concentration
State vs memory

State vs unarmed citizen
wounded by no foreign blast nor shell

forced into the sick-field
brains-out coughing downwind

backing into the alley   hands shielding eyes
under glare-lit choppers coming through   low

3

In the dream you—is it?—set down
two packages in brown paper

saying, *Without such means*
*there can be no end*

*to the wrenching of mind*
*from body, the degradation*

*no end to everything you hate*
*and have exposed, lie upon lie*

I think: *We've been dying slowly*
*now we'll be blown to bits*

I think you're testing me
*"how vitally we desired disaster"*

You say, *there can be no poetry*
*without the demolition*

*of language, no end to everything you hate*
*lies upon lies*

•

I think: you're testing me
testing us both

but isn't this what it means to live—
pushing further the conditions in which we breathe?

4

In the college parlor by the fireplace
ankled and waisted with bells

he, inclined by nature toward tragic themes
chants of the eradication of tribal life

in a blue-eyed trance
shaking his neckbent silvering hair

Afterward, wine and cake at the Provost's house

and this is surely no dream, how the beneficiary
of atrocities yearns toward innocence

and this is surely a theme, the vengeful rupture
of prized familiar ways

and calculated methods
for those who were there     But for those elsewhere

it's something else, not herds hunted down cliffs
maybe a buffalo burger in the

tribal college cafeteria
and computer skills after lunch     Who wants to be tragic?

The college coheres out of old quonset huts
demolition-scavenged doors, donated labor

used textbooks, no waste, passion
     •

5

Horned blazing fronds of Sierra ice
grow hidden rivulets, last evening's raindrop pulses

in the echeveria's cup next morning, fogdrip darkens the
    road
under fire-naked bishop pines

thick sweats form on skins
of pitched-out nectarines, dumpster shrine

of miracles of truths of mold
Rain streaming, stroking

a broken windowpane
When the story broke I thought

I was thinking about water
how it is most of what we are

and became bottled chic
such thoughts are soon interrupted

6

When the story broke we were trying to think
about history    went on stubbornly thinking

though history plunged
with muddy spurs    screamed at us for trying

to plunder its nest    seize its nestlings
capture tame and sell them or something

after the manner of our kind
Well, was it our secret hope?
                •

—a history you could seize
(as in old folios of "natural history"

each type and order pictured in its place?)
—Back to the shambles, comrades,

where the story is always breaking
down     having to be repaired

7

Under the small plane's fast shadow an autumn
afternoon bends sharply

—swathes of golden membrane, occult blood
seeping up through the great groves

where the intestinal the intestate
blood-cords of the stags are strung from tree to tree

I know already where we're landing
what cargo we'll take on

boxed for the final draping
coming home from home     sewn into its skin

eyes hooded in refusal

—what might be due—

1998–1999

# Architect

*Nothing he had done before*
   *or would try for later*
      will explain or atone
this facile suggestion of crossbeams
languid elevations traced on water
his stake in white colonnades cramping his talent
                    showing up in
facsimile mansions overbearing the neighborhood
his leaving the steel rods out of the plinths
   (bronze raptors gazing from the boxwood)

You could say he spread himself too thin    a plasterer's term
      you could say he was then
skating thin ice    his stake in white colonnades against the
   thinness of
ice itself    a slickened ground
     Could say he did not then love
his art enough to love anything more

Could say he wanted the commission so
badly betrayed those who hired him    an artist
    who in dreams followed
      the crowds who followed him

Imagine commandeering those oversize those prized
   hardwood columns to be hoisted and hung
by hands expert and steady on powerful machines
   his knowledge using theirs as the one kind does the
                other (as it did in Egypt)
     •

—while devising the little fountain to run all night
   outside the master bedroom

1998–1999


# Fox

I needed fox    Badly I needed
a vixen for the long time none had come near me
I needed recognition from a
triangulated face    burnt-yellow eyes
fronting the long body the fierce and sacrificial tail
I needed history of fox    briars of legend it was said she
   had run through
I was in want of fox

And the truth of briars she had to have run through
I craved to feel on her pelt    if my hands could even slide
past or her body slide between them    sharp truth distressing
   surfaces of fur
lacerated skin calling legend to account
a vixen's courage in vixen terms

For a human animal to call for help
on another animal
is the most riven the most revolted cry on earth
come a long way down
Go back far enough it means tearing and torn    endless
   and sudden
back far enough it blurts
into the birth-yell of the yet-to-be human child
pushed out of a female    the yet-to-be woman

1998

# Fire

in the old city    incendiaries abound
who hate this place stuck to their foot soles
Michael Burnhard is being held and I
can tell you about him    pushed-out and living
across the river    low-ground given to flooding
in a shotgun house
his mother working for a hospital
or restaurant    dumpsters    she said a restaurant
hospital cafeteria who cares
what story
you bring home with the food

I can tell you Michael knows beauty
from the frog-iris in mud
the squelch of ankles
stalking the waterlily
the blues beat flung across water from the old city

Michael Burnhard in Black History Month
not his month only he was born there
not black and almost without birthday one
February 29 Michael Burnhard
on the other side of the river
glancing any night at his mother's wrists
crosshatched raw
beside the black-opal stream

Michael Burnhard still beside himself
when fire took the old city
lying like a black spider on its back
under the satellites and a few true stars

1999

# Noctilucent Clouds

Late night on the underside   a spectral glare
abnormal   Everything below
must and will betray itself
as a floodlit truckstop out here
on the North American continent stands revealed
and we're glad because it's late evening and no town
but this, diesel, regular, soda, coffee, chips, beer and video
no government no laws but LIGHT in the continental dark
and then   and then   what smallness the soul endures
rolling out on the ramp from such an isle
onto the harborless Usonian plateau

Dear Stranger   can I raise a poem
to justice   you not here
with your sheet-lightning apprehension
of nocturne
your surveyor's eye for distance
as if any forest's fallen tree were for you
a possible hypotenuse

Can I wake as I once woke with no thought of you
into the bad light of a futureless motel

This thing I am calling justice:
I could slide my hands into your leather gloves
but my feet would not fit into your boots

Every art leans on some other:   yours
on mine in spasm retching
last shreds of vanity
We swayed together like cripples when the wind
suddenly turned a corner   or was it we who turned

•

Once more I invite you into this
*in retrospect it will be clear*

1999


# If Your Name Is on the List

If your name is on the list of judges
you're one of them
though you fought their hardening
assumptions     went and stood
alone by the window while they
concurred
It wasn't enough to hold your singular
minority opinion
You had to face the three bridges
down the river
your old ambitions
flamboyant in bloodstained mist

You had to carry off under arm
and write up in perfect loneliness
your soul-splitting dissent

Yes, I know a soul can be partitioned like a country
In all the new inhere old judgments
loyalties crumbling send up sparks and smoke
We want to be part of the future     dragging in
what pure futurity can't use

Suddenly a narrow street a little beach a little century
screams     *Don't let me go*
                   •

*Don't let me die   Do you forget*
*what we were to each other*

1999


# 1999

Before the acute
point of the severing
I wanted to see into my century's
hinged and beveled mirror
clear of smoke
eyes of coal and ruby
stunned neck the carrier of bricks and diamonds
brow of moonlit oyster shells
barbed wire lacework disgracing
the famous monument

Behind it spread the old
indigenous map    landscape
before conquerors    horizon ownless

# Four Short Poems

1

*(driving home from Robin Blaser's reading)*

The moon
is not romantic.   No.   It's
a fact of life and still
we aren't inured. You would think, it reflects
the waves not draws them.    So
I'd compel you as I
have been compelled by you.   On the coast road
between drafts of fog
that face (and yes, it is
expressioned) breaking in and out
doth speak to us
as he did in his courtliness
and operatic mystery.

2

We're not yet out of the everglades
     of the last century
          our body parts are still there

though we would have our minds careen and swoop
     over the new ocean
          *with a wild surmise*

the bloody strings
     tangled and stuck between
          become our lyre
               •

3

Beethoven's "Appassionata" played on a parlor grand
    piano
in a small California town by a boy from Prague
here for a month to learn American
This is not "The Work of Art in the Age of Mechanical
    Reproduction"
This is one who startles the neighbors with his owning
of the transmissible heritage one evening
then for the whole month droops over the Internet.

4

From the new crudities, from the old
apartheid spraying ruin on revolution,
back to Du Bois of Great Barrington and Africa

or Kafka of the intransmissible
tradition
the stolen secrets in the cleft

reside   and this, beloved poets
is where our hearts, livers and lights still
dwell unbeknownst and vital

                    *for Elizabeth Willis and for Peter Gizzi*

2000

# Ends of the Earth

All that can be unknown is stored in the black screen of a
    broken television set.
Coarse-frosted karst crumbling as foam, eel eyes piercing
    the rivers.
Dark or light, leaving or landfall, male or female demarca-
    tions dissolve
into the O of time and solitude. I found here: no inter/
ruption to a version of earth so abandoned and abandoning
I read it my own acedia lashed by the winds
questing shredmeal toward the Great Plains, that ocean. My
    fear.

Call it Galisteo but that's not the name of what happened
    here.

If indoors in an eyeflash (perhaps) I caught the gazer of spaces
lighting the two wax candles in black iron holders
against the white wall after work and after dark
but never saw the hand

how inhale the faint mist of another's gazing, pacing, dozing
words muttered aloud in utter silence, gesture unaware
thought that has suffered and borne itself to the ends of
    the earth
web agitating between my life and another's?
Other whose bed I have shared but never at once together?

2000

# Notes

## THE DIAMOND CUTTERS

*The Snow Queen.* Hans Christian Andersen's tale was the point of departure.

## SNAPSHOTS OF A DAUGHTER-IN-LAW

*Snapshots of a Daughter-in-Law.* The lines in Part 7 beginning "To have in this uncertain world some stay" were written by Mary Wollstonecraft in *Thoughts on the Education of Daughters* (London, 1787).

## NECESSITIES OF LIFE

*In the Woods.* The first line is borrowed and translated from the Dutch poet, J. C. Bloem.

*"I Am in Danger—Sir—."* See *The Letters of Emily Dickinson.* Thomas Johnson and Theodora Ward, eds., Vol. 2 (Cambridge: Harvard University Press, 1958), p. 409.

## LEAFLETS

*Orion.* One or two phrases suggested by Gottfried Benn's essay, "Artists and Old Age," in *Primal Vision: Selected Writings,* ed. E. B. Ashton. (New York: New Directions, 1960).

*For a Russian Poet.* Part 3 is based on an account by the poet Natalya Gorbanevskaya of a protest action against the Soviet invasion of Czechoslovakia. Gorbanevskaya was later held, and bore a child, in a "penal mental institution" for her political activities.

*Leaflets.* "The love of a fellow-creature in all its fullness consists simply in the ability to say to him, 'What are you going through?'" —Simone Weil.

*Ghazals: Homage to Ghalib.* This poem began to be written after I read Aijaz Ahmad's literal English versions of the Urdu poetry of Mirza Ghalib (1797–1869). While the structure and metrics of the classical *ghazal* form used by Ghalib are much stricter than mine, I adhered to his use of a minimum five couplets to a *ghazal,* each couplet being autonomous and independent of the others. The continuity and unity flow from the associations and images playing back and forth among the couplets in any single *ghazal.* The poems are dated as I wrote them, during a month in the summer of 1968. Although I was a contributor to Ahmad's *The Ghazals of Ghalib* (New York: Columbia University Press, 1971), the *ghazals* here are not translations but original poems.

## UNCOLLECTED POEMS 1950–1974

The first two poems in this section were "lost" for a long time; I had even forgotten their existence. "The Prisoners" first appeared in *The Harvard Advocate,* and "At the Jewish New Year" in *The New Yorker.* "Dien Bien Phu" appeared in *Nimrod.*

*From an Old House in America.* Part 4: The first line is borrowed from Emily Brontë's poem, "Stanzas."
    Part 7: Many African women went into labor and gave birth on the slave-ships of the Middle Passage, chained for the duration of the voyage to the dying or the dead.
    Part 11: *Datura* is a poisonous hallucinogenic weed with a spiky green pod and a white flower; also known as jimson-weed, or deadly nightshade.

## A WILD PATIENCE HAS TAKEN ME THIS FAR

*Grandmothers.* Part 3: Italicized lines are quoted from Lillian Smith, *Killers of the Dream* (New York: Norton, 1961), p. 39.

*The Spirit of Place.* Italicized passages in Part 3 are from *The Letters of Emily Dickinson,* Thomas Johnson and Theodora Ward, eds. (Cambridge: Harvard University Press, 1958), specifically, from Letter 154 to Susan Gilbert (June 1854) and Letter 203 to Catherine Scott Anthon Turner (March 1859).

## YOUR NATIVE LAND, YOUR LIFE

*North American Time.* Julia de Burgos (1914–1953): Puerto Rican poet and revolutionary, who died on the streets of New York City.

*Contradictions.* 26: See Cynthia Ozick, *Art and Ardor* (New York: Farrar, Straus & Giroux, 1984), p. 255: "the glorious So What: the life-cry."

27: Ding Ling, leading Chinese novelist and major literary figure in the Revolutionary government under Mao. Exiled in 1957 for writing too critically and independently. Imprisoned as a counterrevolutionary in 1970; cleared of all charges in 1976 at the end of the Cultural Revolution.

## TIME'S POWER

*The Desert as Garden of Paradise.* Section 2: Chavela Vargas, a Mexican popular and traditional singer.

Section 3: Malintzin/La Malinche/Marina are names for an Aztec woman given as a slave to Hernán Cortés on his arrival in Mexico in 1519. Her historical reality has undergone many layerings of legend and symbolism; more recently she has become a frequent presence in Chicana feminist literature. See, for example, Norma Alarcón, "Chicana's Feminist Literature: A Revision through Malintzin," in *This*

*Bridge Called My Back: Writings by Radical Women of Color,* ed. Gloria Anzaldúa and Cherríe Moraga (Latham, N.Y.: Kitchen Table/Women of Color Press). See also Lucha Corpi's "Marina" poems, and the author's note, in *Fireflight: Three Latin American Poets,* trans. Catherine Rodriguez-Nieto (Oakland, Calif.: Oyez Books, 1975); and Gloria Anzaldúa, *Borderlands: La Frontera: The New Mestiza* (San Francisco: Spinsters/Aunt Lute Books, 1987).

Section 7: See Peter Masten Dunne, S.J., *Black Robes in Lower California* (Berkeley: University of California Press, 1968); Antonine Tibeson, O.F.M., ed., *The Writings of Junípero Serra,* I (Washington, D.C.: Academy of American Franciscan History, 1955); Robert F. Heizer, ed., *The Destruction of California Indians* (Santa Barbara and Salt Lake City: Peregrine Smith, 1974); Van H. Garner, *The Broken Ring: The Destruction of the California Indians* (Tucson, Ariz.: Westernlore Press, 1982).

Sections 10, 11: Italicized phrases from John C. van Dyke, *The Desert* (1901) (Salt Lake City: Peregrine Smith, 1980).

*Harpers Ferry.* In 1859, the white abolitionist John Brown rented a farm near Harpers Ferry, Virginia (now West Virginia), as a base for slave insurrections. On October 16 of that year, he and his men raided and captured the federal arsenal, but found their escape blocked by local militia; the U.S. Marines then seized the arsenal. Ten of Brown's men were killed in this conflict, and Brown himself was later tried and hanged.

Harriet Tubman (1820–1913), Black antislavery activist and strategist, led more than 300 people from slavery to freedom via the Underground Railroad. She was known as "General Moses." Though in contact with John Brown, she withdrew from participation before the raid. Tubman never actually came to Harpers Ferry; her appearance in this poem is a fiction.

## AN ATLAS OF THE DIFFICULT WORLD

*An Atlas of the Difficult World.* V: "over the chained bay waters." From Hart Crane, "To Brooklyn Bridge," in *The Poems of Hart Crane,* ed. Marc Simon (New York and London: Liveright, 1989; poem originally published in 1930). "There are roads to take when you think of your country." From Muriel Rukeyser, *U. S. 1* (New York: Covici Friede, 1938); see also Muriel Rukeyser, *The Collected Poems* (New York: McGraw-Hill, 1978). "I don't want to know how he tracked them." On May 13, 1988, Stephen Roy Carr shot and killed Rebecca Wight, one of two lesbians camping on the Appalachian Trail in Pennsylvania. Her lover, Claudia Brenner, suffered five bullet wounds. She dragged herself two miles along the trail to a road, where she flagged a car to take her to the police. In October of that year, Carr was found guilty of first-degree murder and sentenced to life in prison without parole. During the legal proceedings, it became clear that Carr had attacked the women because they were lesbians. See *Gay Community News* (August 7 and November 11, 1988).

X: The passages in italics are quoted from *Soledad Brother: The Prison Letters of George Jackson* (New York: Bantam, 1970), pp. 24, 26, 93, 245.

*Tattered Kaddish.* "The Reapers of the Field are the Comrades, masters of this wisdom, because *Malkhut* is called the Apple Field, and She grows sprouts of secrets and new meanings of Torah. Those who constantly create new interpretations of Torah are the ones who reap Her" (Moses Cordovero, Or ha-Hammah on Zohar III, 106a). See Barry W. Holtz, ed., *Back to the Sources: Reading the Classic Jewish Texts* (New York: Summit, 1984), p. 305.

## DARK FIELDS OF THE REPUBLIC

*What Kind of Times Are These.* The title is from Bertolt Brecht's poem "An Die Nachgeborenen" ("For Those Born Later"): *What kind of times are these / When it's almost a crime to talk about trees / Because it means keeping still about so many evil deeds?* (For the complete poem, in a different translation, see John Willett and Ralph Manheim, eds., *Bertolt Brecht, Poems 1913–1956* [New York: Methuen, 1976], pp. 318–320.)

"our country moving closer to its own truth and dread . . ." echoes Osip Mandelstam's 1921 poem that begins *I was washing outside in the darkness* and ends *The earth's moving closer to truth and to dread.*

(Clarence Brown and W. S. Merwin, trans., *Osip Mandelstam: Selected Poems* [New York: Atheneum, 1974], p. 40.) Mandelstam was forbidden to publish, then exiled and sentenced to five years of hard labor for a poem caricaturing Stalin; he died in a transit camp in 1938.

*Calle Visión.* Calle Visión is the name of a road in the southwestern United States—literally, "Vision Street."

1: "that tells the coming of the railroad." "With the coming of the railroad, new materials and pictorial designs and motifs, including trains themselves, appeared in Navaho weaving (ca. 1880)." (From the Museum of Indian Arts and Culture, Museum of New Mexico, Santa Fe.)

3: "a place not to live but to die in." See Sir Thomas Browne, *Religio Medici* (1635): "For the World, I count it not an Inn, but an Hospital; and a place not to live, but to dye in." (*Religio Medici and Other Writings by Sir Thomas Browne* [London: Everyman's Library, J. M. Dent, 1947], p. 83.)

4: "Have you ever worked around metal? . . ." From a questionnaire filled out before undergoing a magnetic resonance imaging (MRI) scan.

"The world is falling down . . . ." From the song "The World Is Falling Down," composed by Abbey Lincoln, sung by her on the Verve recording of the same title, 1990 (Moseka Music BMI).

5: "And the fire shall try . . . ." I Corinthians 3:13: "Every man's work shall be made manifest . . . and the fire shall try every man's work of what sort it is." Used by Studs Terkel as an epigraph to his *Working* (New York: Pantheon, 1974).

*Then or Now.* This sequence of poems derives in part from Hannah Arendt and Karl Jaspers, *Correspondence 1926–1969,* ed. Lotte and Hans Saner, trans. Robert and Rita Kimbel (New York: Harcourt Brace Jovanovich, 1992). While reading these letters, I had been reflecting on concepts of "guilt" and "innocence" among artists and intellectuals like myself in the United States. The poems owe much also to the continuing pressure of events.

*Late Ghazal.* See "Ghazals (Homage to Ghalib)" and "The Blue Ghazals," in Adrienne Rich, *Collected Early Poems: 1950–1970* (New

York: Norton, 1993), pp. 339–355, 368–372. See also Aijaz Ahmad, ed., *Ghazals of Ghalib* (New York: Columbia University Press, 1971).

*Inscriptions.* "Two: movement": "I need to live each day through . . . ." These two lines are quoted from an earlier poem of mine ("8/8/68: I") in "Ghazals (Homage to Ghalib)"; see above.

"Four:history": "When shall we learn, what should be clear as day, . . . .?" These two lines are from W. H. Auden's "Canzone," in *The Collected Poetry of W. H. Auden* (New York: Random House, 1945), p. 161.

"Six: edgelit": "Medbh's postcard from Belfast." I thank the Northern Irish poet Medbh McGuckian for permission to quote her words from a postcard received in August 1994.

"suffused / by what it works in, 'like the dyer's hand.'" I had written "suffused," later began looking up the line I was quoting from memory: was it Coleridge? Keats? Shakespeare? My friend Barbara Gelpi confirmed it was Shakespeare, in his Sonnet III: *Thence comes it that my name receives a brand / And almost thence my nature is subdued / To what it works in, like the dyer's hand.* I have kept "suffused" here because to feel *suffused* by the materials that one has perforce to work in is not necessarily to be *subdued,* though some might think so.

## MIDNIGHT SALVAGE

*Char.* Italicized phrases and some images from *Leaves of Hypnos,* the journal kept in 1942–1943 by the poet René Char while he was a commander in the French Resistance, and from some of Char's poems. I have drawn on both Jackson Mathews's and Cid Corman's translations of Char's journal in integrating his words into my poem. Char joined the Surrealist movement late and broke with it prior to World War II. It was André Breton who said, "The simplest surrealist act consists of going down into the street, revolver in hand, and shooting at random."

*Camino Real.* "Can you afford not to make / the magical study / which happiness is?" From Charles Olson, "Variations Done for Gerald Van der Wiele," in *Charles Olson, Selected Poems,* ed. Robert Creeley (Berkeley: University of California Press, 1997), p. 83.

"George Oppen to June Degnan: . . ." See *The Selected Letters of George Oppen,* ed. Rachel Blau DuPlessis (Durham, N.C.: Duke University Press, 1990), p. 212.


## FOX


*Noctilucent Clouds.* "Several times in the last few months, observers in the lower 48 have seen 'noctilucent clouds,' which develop about 50 miles above the earth's surface—clouds so high that they reflect the sun's rays long after nightfall. . . . [G]lobal warming seems to be driving them toward the equator. . . . In retrospect it will be clear." Bill McKibben, "Indifferent to a Planet in Pain," *New York Times,* Saturday, 4 September 1999, sec. A.

"Usonian": The term used by Frank Lloyd Wright for his prairie-inspired American architecture.

# Index